AF887321

FAUST

A Re-Creation of the Legend

by Stuart McCarrell

with dramatic structure
from Goethe's *Faust* Part I

XENIA

XENIA DRAMA SERIES
1564 N. Damen Avenue
Chicago, IL 60622

XENIA PRESS
1564 N. Damen Avenue
Chicago, IL 60622
FAX # (312) 772-2003

Printed in the U.S.A.

10 9 8 7 6 5 4 3 2 1

ISBN: 1-880001-03-9

On Faust, Goethe, and translation—or why this re-creation was necessary

Goethe's Faust (Part 1) is a tragic and poignant love story that is at the same time a passionate meditation on "What is man?" Deep and subtle asides on philosophy, psychology, and politics are perfectly blended with savage satire and ribald humor. But the main characters are three-dimensional and their story exists and moves us on its own level. The overtones are endless.

Yet this greatest of plays has never existed as a viable play in English. The best translation, by far, is Bayard Taylor's of 1871. Taylor is particularly strong in "high points"--the songs and major speeches. His secret is that, though he is a minor poet himself, he so completely devotes himself to Goethe that the results of his work far exceed that of men like MacNiece and Jarrell, who are somewhat better poets. Unfortunately, these latter two approach Goethe and his masterpiece with such light-hearted and light-headed academic arrogance that their translations are almost worthless.

But this play is often and well performed in Germany. It is of immense world-wide prestige. Why have no British or American writers succeeded in bringing it alive into English? I think there are three reasons:

1/ Goethe is first of all a supreme lyric poet. Lyric poetry is by definition the poetry that almost never translates well. A large part of the appeal of this play to modern Germans lies in the sheer beauty of the songs and the complex and ever-varying counterpoint of the speeches.

2/ The medieval legends, the witchcraft, and the magic settings and actions of the play are strange and distancing (in an unhealthy sense) to English and American audiences. To Germans these images out of their past have a resonance (partly because of Goethe and his play) that they do not have for us. It is true that we can "suspend disbelief" to some extent—as modern Germans do also. But every suspension of disbelief in a literary work is at the cost of a certain amount of psychic energy. This loss coupled with the loss of the music in translation kills the immediacy on which every play relies.

3/ Most of the translators have had little or no comprehension of the full scope and grandeur of Goethe and his achievement. Taylor and Walter Kaufmann are the exceptions. But Kaufmann, powerful mind that he is, is no poet. So his "existential" translation fails. However, almost all the comments in his introduction are both profound and vital.

For six generations now, dozens of translators of every degree of skill and dedication have tried and failed to do justice to this play. That fact, coupled with points number 1 and 2 from above lead me to conclude that Shakespeare himself could not bring Goethe's *Faust* alive *as a translation*. What is needed to give new life to this great prototype of all dramas is what was needed for Homer's great prototype of all novels (and which Joyce furnished): a new set of "objective correlatives," a restatement of the eternal questions, a recreation of the splendid characters—in modern terms. That is what I have tried to achieve here. The writing took three years. The rewriting took four and one half years. The rewriting consisted of trying to eliminate any shadow of rhetoric or filler; and of trying to put poetic energy into each line so that the actor would look forward to speaking it. Did I succeed? The book is in your hands. You judge.

Stuart McCarrell Chicago, May 1992

FAUST

FAUST

Cast List (in order of Appearance)

	FIRST APPEARANCE
RAPHAEL	iv
GABRIEL	iv
MICHAEL	iv
MEPHISTOPHELES	iv
GOD	v
FAUST	1
Zen Master	6
WAGNER	7
Several Students	17
Other Students	17
Young Townsman	17
1st, 2nd, 3rd, 4th, 5th Student	17
Working Girl	17
1st Girl, 2nd Girl	18
Expensively Dressed Girl	18
Citizen	19
Tramp	19
Another Citizen	19
Third Citizen	19
Gypsy	19
Athletes (singing)	20
Young People Dancing	22
Old Workman	23
SMITH	31
Young Woman in Yellow	42
STUDENT	50
GUY	58
MIKE	58
PAUL	58
DAN	58
MONOHAM	71
SHOCKLEE	71
WARTHOG	71
JEAN HEX	72
PALM	75
PEGGY	81
MARTHA	93
Liz	127
CRAIG	130
M.C. (Studs Terkel)	138

(cont.)

SONGS

For Goethe

(Preface to a re-creation of Faust)

Through births, and blooming, and bitterness and blood,
across subtle systems and the moon-swelled tide,
through betrayals, victories, tender long loves,
old master, I've wandered—and stayed at your side.

Two centuries between us—Tolstoy, Marx,
Einstein, Mars—man's true history begun.
Master, we have no more masters or worship
except humanity, reason, nature, sun.

For those you wove, wrangled, gave half your life. I've only
taken your fable and shaken out the dust—
superstitions you used—we're older now.
Our devils need no magic—just blind trust.

Your idealism I've made material and hard.
You dialectic is there; Man— the spark, the clay—
dreams, defines himself in work, and dies.
Goethe, I have been true to you in my way.

FOUR ILLUMINATED POSTERS AGAINST THE WALLS OF THE THEATRE

In its proper meaning, dialectics is the study of the contradiction *within the very essence of things.*

Lenin

His (Satan's) goal, which the magic and cynicism of Mephisto serves, is the bestialization of man, the creation of a "spiritual animal kingdom." (Hegel)

George Lukacs

I think I could turn and live with animals, they are so
placid and self-contained.
I stand and look at them long and long.
They do not sweat and whine about their condition;
They do not lie awake in the dark and weep for their sins;
They do not make me sick discussing their duty to God;
Not one is dissatisfied—not one is demented with the
 mania of owning things;
Not one kneels to another, nor to his kind that lived
 thousands of years ago;
Not one is respectable or industrious over the whole earth.

Whitman

For the Lord's thesis is that evil is a mistake, and not the inevitable concomitant of human nature...Mephisto, on the contrary, contends that the human race...does not know the meaning of the word evil and can be led into it and out of it like a lot of silly acquiescent sheep...Not one man stands in the dock: this is the trial of the human race itself.

D. J. Enright

How could man live at all if he did not give absolution every night to himself and all his brothers?

Goethe

Another feature of the play that approximates perfection is the craftsmanship of the construction. We seem to be confronted with "epic theatre" over a hundred years before Bert Brecht.

Walter Kaufmann

My young friend, theory is dry and gray.
But life is sweet and glad on any day.

Smith

DEDICATION

Misty dreams of youth, you come again
like memories of love, all sun, all pain.
I say, "This time I'll get it down,"
still playing the hopeful, brokenhearted clown.
You rule half my life. You want the weird power
of the dead more tangible than flesh.
I become a yearning boy. My joys go sour—
You trap me in some tragic, sacred mesh...

You're just agonies and delights from childhood,
shadows, caresses that haunt my sleep:
first love, and friendship, and the fevered blood—
then why must I wake myself or weep?
You're just pain. Always that tortured tune
from the labyrinth of life. Just pain
for those who died in golden, careless June.
No tears erase or fade that obscene stain.

Beyond my touch or voice, those with whom I read
poems, drank, heard music when young
are scattered like storm-struck birds. I work instead
for strangers. Even if they throng
about and cheer—it's not the same.
I bring songs to those I hardly know,
wanting them to care—but longing for one name
from yesterday with its Indian summer glow.

Always the dark, half-buried desires win.
I live with shadows, mighty and serene.
My fingers trace the memory of their skin—
my talk is their destruction and their sheen.
I shiver, I weep, my pride is gone—
no use the aimless rushing, or the manly poise.
What is around me is unreal and I'm alone
with what I've lost, its piercing sweetness, its lovely noise.

PROLOGUE IN HEAVEN
Song of the Archangels

RAPHAEL
The sun, source of all and speck of dust,
heedless, pre-determined, wild,
spinning forever once begun,
in spiral filaments, trackless, endless...
Awe and wonderment to man,
creation flaming, silent, raucous,
is bright and perfect now as then.

GABRIEL
And swift beyond conception swift
the strangeness of the universe weaves on—
Light into blackness, blackness to flame,
terror and glory all in one.

MICHAEL
The sea storms rip against the land
and back again against the sea. One chain
all savage crashing force.
Yet God, how soft
the winds revive the April plain
and how serene the smallest hill
blooms and summers to your will.

CHORUS
The exploding star systems rage,
black yet blazing, massive/empty...
mocking measurements and man.
Wild, changeless, old creation
is pitiless and perfect now as then.
Lord, Lord, each clear voice must praise
how terrifying, how tender are your ways.

MEPHISTOPHELES *[to God]*
You'll forgive me, old professor,
if I've learned everything—except respect.

MEPHISTOPHELES (continued)
These "singers" give me pain
in both ass and neck. Whoever has a nagging wife should bless her.
He can learn from derision and disdain.
But sugar tongues insult your brain.
Theirs is the real, the broad view they insist.
"Broad view." I love it from below.
There's the source. The heaven to be kissed—
Don't scowl (the old stiff nose with your heart of snow),
men have many pleasures you can't know.

I keep a watch on man—his half-wit habits.
He's the apple of your eye, the plum, the peach.
This offshoot of baboons and rabbits
has his "god" to dream of. God—his tender reach,
his sparrow caring eye, and endless mercy.
Meantime he drags his sister in the ditch.

For he has "reason." That's the added feature.
He cooks up reasons for his every move.
From *You* he gets permits to kill
given by fat rabbis, ministers, puling priests,
who bless each army as it trudges to the slaughter.
Then they race home to mumble at some feast.
Reason? Religion? I'll take the honest glut of beasts.

GOD
Is that your same old speech?
That's all you see? All? That's
your squinting vision? That's your crippled reach?

MEPHISTOPHELES
That's all there is—if one is honest.
I walk among 'em—narrow, nagging town; cold, crafty city.
Their misery almost moves my pity.

GOD
You know Faust?

MEPHISTOPHELES
The dreamer? Dr. Faust. The wild one!

GOD
A solid, sober man. My follower.

MEPHISTOPHELES
Strange follower. He's not content with earthly women, food, drink.
His soul is loose—out on the moor,
or behind the moon. I sometimes think
it's Helen of Troy or *some* famous whore
he's after. I sometimes think it's you
he wants to be. And sometimes
in a cold, revenge-mad rage—it's me.

GOD
He may be confused but his heart is good.
I see the process, the fragile sun-seeking tender buds, the future tree.
Living will lead him back to me.

MEPHISTOPHELES
I'd bet my balls and blood against that. He'll come to me
if you refrain from force and terror.
Let him choose between us.
Let him be free!

GOD
As long as he's alive he's free.
He has his own desires and needs.
It's fullness of them that honors me.
Frostbitten and fruitless are your sorry seeds.

MEPHISTOPHELES
We have a wager. These lusty ones I want. You
can stack up the dullards and count them twice.
I'll play for the active ones, alert, awake.
You keep the plump, sleepy church mice.

GOD
You have the chance. Convince him,
turn him around. Dazzle him. Lie.
Lead him to curse humanity. Then
like a sick, snow-blinded sheep he'll die.
But I say you will lose. Hurt
and lonely, he'll still struggle
to find me—the pattern, the purpose…

MEPHISTOPHELES
I'll win this bet and break his fickle will.
Always in his dreams he belongs to me,
lying, cheating, swimming around in swill.
He hates half-knowing, being half-way free.
He wants the jungle again, the honest animal choice—
not insults and curses—from some imaginary voice.

GOD
You're free to do the worst you can.
Your kind has never moved my hate.
Man's wild nature soon leaves him tired.
By thirty he'd sit around and wait.
But your agitation keeps him active. I conspired
with his own needs, and nature and chance.
You and confusion and greed are part of the dance.
[to the Archangels and/or the audience]
But you who already know the deeper beauty—
hold hard to it! Enjoy. Love. Praise.
Help it become real for everyone,
to everyone. Make that the purpose of your days.

MEPHISTOPHELES *[to the audience]*
I don't mind talking to the old one.
He doesn't impress me very much.
He's quite civil and decent—
for a ruler. And, of course, he's out of touch.

SCENE 1
Faust's Study
SOUTHERN CALIFORNIA

A large, well-furnished study. It is midnight. There is a large picture window that looks out onto a scene, part rural and part urban.

Faust paces restlessly. He may drink occasionally—what and how, to the director's taste. It is the mood and feeling that are important. Faust is a very intelligent, very serious, very disturbed man. He is at a turning point in his life. The year is 1970.

FAUST
I've studied philosophy, medicine, law,
even religion—deeply. And here I stand—
hollow, restless, with anger in my craw—
a would-be lover in a lifeless land.
I'm a doctor and department head.
For ten years students have come to study here
and I've played along, I've led
'em by the nose—to nowhere.
All that I know myself that matters
is that life and death are vast and real
and our knowledge, ink-stained scraps and tatters
that can do much harm—but cannot heal.
I think I'm above the phonies and fops
who run our little learned rackets,
tagging behind the murderous rulers with mops
and soap: "programs" in sealed official packets.
But I have no pleasure or real work.
The conventional wisdom brought up to date,
that's the brackish bilge I bring. I can't help
a student find out what to love—or hate.
And what's my reward for drag-ass drudgery?
Tenure! To watch and help ideals and passions fade.
To give up life, travel, adventure…
[He goes to the window.]

FAUST (continued)
I need the touch of flesh, I need to wade
back into the sweet fountains, the source;
to break the hold of mind and empty phrases,
to feel again the wonder, the primal force.
The lucky ones live direct and sing its praises
in their simple lusts and loves. They live
in a warmer, wilder world than mine.
What drives them drives the sun. I walk
a priggish, programmed, anti-human line.
There's the moon again. How many years
have I watched that silver ball float free
and steady in the black and empty sky?
Empty? That reflects my life and me.
Oh, God, to think of who else that light
lies soft upon this second: the lovers
on a thousand beaches, tossing, sleeping;
campers in the mountains, the hand hovers,
teases, touches the waiting breast. Even weeping
and suffering is better than this bookish room.
To be outside and wild with the moon
is the way to live—to laugh at doom.
[He walks among his tables and bookcases.]
Instead this is mine—these heaps of thought,
these pictures of love, these painted idols.
Each one a token of a battle fought
and won or lost, honorably, dangerously.
Each one to me a souvenir that ought
to shame me or any man who tries
to buy another's wounds and thinks with pride
they're his by title transfer. These shallow lies
we feed each other, we flabby ones who hide
from human life and call our cringing "objective studies."
Like frogs in a stagnant pond, we shove for sun,
we grunt and push each other down—the water muddies.

Is it any wonder that I'm restless?
At forty still to be at children's games:
[He goes back to the window.]

Turner

Faust: "To be outside and wild with the moon..."

FAUST (continued)
and indoor games at that. God knows
[He opens the window.]
it is not winter. It is fear that lames
the likes of me. The rest of mankind
lives in the open. I have the mighty dead
for companions and lovers. They lived with fiery hearts
and fevered blood. My life is in my head.

But here is Buddha. Here is escape.
This single volume breaks the iron chain
that Western man has carried
so long he thinks his very pain
is part of nature. In this old wisdom
is peace and happiness if I can find
the will not to will. If I give up
the arrogance. If I can grasp what binds
the universe in a seamless, perfect web.
I'm ready to change my life. Right here
is the deepest, hardest, yet most simple
way—to cast out vanity—and fear.
[He picks up and thumbs through Alan Watt's The Way of Zen.*]*
What knowledge deeper than thought!
My body feels it—I come alive.
I remember by letting go of "ought"
or "should." What fools we are to strive
for control when we are a part
of the sweet, slow universe that flows
and never questions or fears. There is no start
or finish. The river neither stays nor goes.
It is. The sun is in it. The birds
and it and I are music that rises
and falls. How foolish our divisive words.
What madness our battles and our yearly crisis.
"The Taos principle is spontaneity,
Cut out cleverness and there are no anxieties…
People in general are so happy, as if enjoying a feast

FAUST (continued)
or as going up to a tower in Spring."
A tower in spring—what memories rush
upon my frozen heart. I was a boy,
I lived and played. There was the flush
of youth and fantasy—the steady joy
of life not separate from flowers and dogs.
I ran, the wind chased me. I slept,
the trees waited or sent fingers, fogs—
or frost to etch wonder on cold glass. I wept
for fallen birds, for tangible creatures.
Now those wolves, pain and death, are gaining fast.
They've become my blind guides, my savage teachers.
Like leaves we can't rest, or escape, or last...
[He reads again, intently.]
Yet this wisdom draws me in.
Here is the answer and the strength.
Music out of anguish. I could be drunk.
I feel the symmetry. I love the length—
and brevity of life. Nothing can stop
what's flowing in me now.
The tides of luck can come or go.
No more asking why or how.
[Sitting on the floor, arms around his knees, he rocks himself slowly.]
Calm is on me,
the room fades out.
Everything is changed.
I'm seeing for the first time.
I'm touching again.
This time I'll not turn back.
This is reality *[touches a vase]*
and this *[touches a lamp]*.
God, I feel the weight
and beauty
of things!
Da.
Da.
Da.
Om, Om, Om.

[He is in a trance-like state. The following scene is either a memory or a dream—or part of both. A Zen master in white appears. He is very slight, very slim, and very dignified. He looks toward the dreaming Faust but the voice of Faust comes from offstage and is not quite natural.]

ZEN MASTER
You are here again, Dr. Faust?

FAUST
It is not easy for me to come.

ZEN MASTER
You have come to us many times.
You have studied and questioned.
And now…

FAUST
I can't. I can't.

ZEN MASTER
Our wisdom has been your desire;
my voice, my teaching, your consolation.
Here I am. How predictable
your qualms. Where is the questing Dr. Faust?
Where is the anguished man who cried, "Enough"?
Who turned his back on all
weird creeds, wrong turns, wranglings of Western man.
Are you the one ready for inner peace,
who came to us for instruction?
Now full of quibbles and doubts?

FAUST
It is so difficult, so complex.
I want to reconcile both…

ZEN MASTER *[chants]*
All is simple in life's wave.
All is needed—
all you crave.
Flower dead is flower seeded.
Nothing is yours in all that flowing.
You are one with all that glowing.
For us there is no complexity,
nothing to be reconciled because nothing
is ever separate.

FAUST
Your wisdom is deep and true.
I accept it—

ZEN MASTER
It cannot be accepted or willed. You
will never be one of us.

[A knock starts at Faust's door, soft at first but gradually louder. Faust starts to waken; the Zen Master disappears.]

FAUST
No! No!
I can...
I want...
[Knocking is very loud and Faust is fully awake.]
GODDAMN! *[looks at his watch]*
I try to grow wise.
Not much chance this term.
It's that pest with watery eyes.
[He goes to the door and admits Wagner, a young (younger than Faust, at any rate) instructor in Faust's department. He has on slacks and a loud sport shirt.]

WAGNER
It seemed that shadows moved—I heard voices—I thought;
we'll talk about my thesis—-its title, my theme is,

WAGNER (continued)
"Communication and Communion for Commuters".
It's full of formulas and facts. My scheme is
that our religious—no all our leaders ought
to study shows and showmen. Will that be bought?

FAUST
They'd all be mimes or classic comics with no strain.
If they could steal heart, guts—and a brain.

WAGNER
Well, they must prepare their programs shut away
so they only meet the great mass of men
in crowds at rallies or on a holiday.
Yet they must tell them what to do and when.

FAUST
It can't be done. No argument or art
changes anyone or matters—unless it's clear,
helpful, human hunger from one who's part
of the agony and work of those who hear.
The paid liar patches platitudes and tries
to find beauty in brute force, or play on fears.
He's peddling what money always buys.
But soon the smiles shrivel to sickly leers.
The applause is from frauds who sit above
and always seek the sycophant and fake.
Your hope, and honesty, and the people's love
come from caring and risking 'til you break.

WAGNER
Yet much depends upon delivery.
I wish that knack would come to me.

FAUST
Try being selfless and direct.
Avoid the flourishes of a fool.

FAUST (continued)
What's true is wounds, pock-marks, scars. The trick
is making them all part of you.
Then you won't need to juggle words,
or master rhetoric, or learn
the use of body gestures. Forget yourself!
Make contact, care, love, burn
with honor—and work like a mule.
The other way is cleverness, lying—what we teach in school.

WAGNER
But perfect paperwork is also hard.
You have to strain to get it out.
Early Burials and *Tool Chipping* are my life
but I'm tangled in detail each night.
The patching, the patience to prune down
one thought, one phrase! Some nights I lie
and worry that the worst will happen—
before I'm through and satisfied—I'll die.

FAUST
Is it for dusty books you live?
Those pale, mute mimics of blood and breath.
Without involvement—something deep to need and give
life's a stiff, anemic death.

WAGNER
Not for me. I love to dredge up old quotes
or follow thoughts to their ancient source,
to capture their spirit, sniff around, take notes,
learn all about their historic course.

FAUST
All about indeed—about but never *into*.
The early centuries, my friend, are not
what your scholar friends put down.
The subtle things they've missed, repressed, forgot—
too painful, too difficult, too strange.

FAUST (continued)
So they serve us mostly cold, dry hash—
ideas and struggles trimmed to their own petty range.
Symmetry, simplicity and not the crash
and clang, or the delicate soft webs
that living men once tried to weave—or break.
You call it history. I say it's polished bones—
no warm flesh, no empathy. It's nine-tenths fake.

WAGNER
And yet lost things, the past! The first thoughts and acts.
It's knowledge of them a shallow creature lacks.

FAUST
Knowledge is what we claim we want.
But the little handful who both cared and knew:
like children wise, and innocent, and fresh
they spoke—and felt the quick stroke of the fool
desperate to protect his boss, his pampered flesh.
Stupidity lies everywhere—thick, frozen, cruel.
But Wagner, I'm tired, it's very late.
We'll speak some other time of human fate.

WAGNER
Our talk is always so full and wide,
I wish it could go on all night.
But tomorrow's Easter; maybe you'll decide
to go to town. If it's all right—
we could talk some more—I'll go too.
I want to master every point of view.
[He leaves.]

FAUST
He's the type that never rests,
digging in the earth like greedy ghouls
for gold—they think. Half blind, and deaf, and dumb,
they see a worm that shines and drop their tools.
"I'm rich," they shout. But did he have to come

FAUST (continued)
while I was dreaming of the ancient pools
of acceptance and peace? I was about...
No, to tell the truth, I wasn't ready.
I had tried. I felt again how sweet
their thinking sounds. How deep. How petty
are we who, worshiping power and greed,
grow blind to nature, deaf to human need?

Starting from that. Starting a restless man,
I had studied on and off for years,
trying to still the vanities that fan
our wild hopes—and fuel our wild fears.
I gave up gaudy, glimmering things.
I simplified my life.
Fools clucked, "He loves whatever each day brings,
he's wise—or crazy." But then that jagged knife,
"You will never be one of us."

And he was right, of course.
I had tried. I had worked hard—
was so damn subtle I had tried to force
the temple open. I had starred
in my own ego drama called, "No Ego."
But there was an element of distrust and doubt.
I did not want peace at any price.
I saw among them the "affirming" lout
ignoring the cow dung, the pain, the people's lice.
But in the West it's not just twisted will—
it's all the slow and casual ways we kill.

Whatever starts as generous and brave
soon enough smells of caution and the grave.
Whatever little goals we finally win—
we hoard behind walls so that
warmth and boldness die. Then prating of "sin,"
the lusty, longing boy swells fearful and fat.

FAUST (continued)
It's fear that chews us up and spits us out.
It forces us to wrong choices, wrong careers
where we prod on afraid to think or doubt.
Or care that millions live in pain and tears.

Yes, deeply, I am not a man of calm.
Worry, effort, struggle are my natural bent.
I try to understand, love, control—
chance mocks me—everything seems an accident.
Chances put me here among this pyramided "lore"—
two thousand volumes of brilliant thought.
So brilliant they open some silver door—
to more libraries, more reading until I'm taught
to be either Professor Gush or dear Dr. Snore.
Study, study, study, Faust, you'll learn
by the time you're 70 or maybe 85
that you were once young, and foolish, and alive.
[From a table he picks up and handles a skull.]
This skull is real enough and symbol too
of what matters and of what endures:
the flesh wanted only to live, the flesh turned blue—
the one thing "God" or "human fate" insures.
[He goes back to the shelves.]
These were my studies—liberal, humane.
They were to unravel, cast light, explain
the gold-black soul of man—his crimes
and glories were to be "understood."
But they gave me no answers that hold up.
Truth seems now a quick snake with a hood
that spits and flashes between the sun and shade,
half glimpsed, half imagined—no wonder we're afraid.
[He goes to different shelves.]
My father's truths were here. These heavy books:

FAUST (continued)
Russell, Einstein, Bohr. He loved the hooks,
and cranes, and circuits—and the summer dew
of joy and discovery when physics was innocent.
I often wish I'd followed him.
To start with roots the past has sent
is less painful than to twist and turn by whim
and call it freedom. But roots can die
and leave us lost, alone, and asking, Why?

What draws me to this gun he finally used?
If I were healthy it would not be here.
He hated everything dark, cruel, confused.
He thought science would dry the last human tear.
He worked with Fermi and Oppenheimer—
I remember Taos as a boy—
the desert at sunset, the subtle lovely plants...
They too were part of what he loved—the steady joy
of creation. And then it all went sour:
their thousand midnights meant to stop the beast
created instead a bloody club of power
that strutting cowards used—for their usual feast
of human life—unnecessary, unnecessary.
After Nagasaki he had no will to live.
He was a body—with too much agony to carry—
too much to remember, nothing left to give.

Happiness, to purgatory, to Hell—
one year puts us through the arc.
My mother's illness wasted him as well.
I remember them walking, walking in the dark,
no longer happy, no longer victors—
defeated comrades sharing—not new plans,
but tomorrow's quiet and bitter retreats.
Suffering for more than their own losses—for man's.
One night, she was in the hospital,
I was at school, he took down the gun he hated,
wrote us a long, inevitable letter,

FAUST (continued)
and gave the age the ending either "fated"
or "accidental" that it seemed to need.
The country once alive with hope was choked with weed.
I hung the gun upon this wall
in memory and in defiance of fate.
Now I feel the darkest things that crawl:
How weak is love! How strong is hate!
[He takes the gun down.]
Would it be cowardice or courage?
I can ask the questions now
without the righteousness of youth
or illusions as to why or how
I'm different. How I will escape
the common sorrows that turn to terror
—or jokes if we cease to remember
the honor and dreams of youth—if we cease to care,
and feel. At last, father, I understand.
And I could welcome rest. God, I could welcome rest.
I have loved women, and striving, and whisky,
and friendship, but, finally, sleep is best.
And I could leave now—between loves,
unfair to no one. I could get away
before the worst comes down on me—isolation,
despair. I'd be a fool to stay.

[Faust is handling the gun with increasing nervousness during the last speech. In his pacing he now activates a record player. Naturalness, of course, is all-important in the interweaving of his internal monologue and the songs. His thoughts are not a direct or simple response to the songs—but they are influenced by them. Again it is the mood that is important.]

I will not bear this hollowness...
[The first record starts.]

BLACK, BLACK, BLACK IS THE COLOR
OF MY TRUE LOVE'S HAIR.
HER LIPS ARE SOMETHING WOND'ROUS FAIR.
THE PUREST EYES AND SOFTEST HANDS,
I LOVE THE GROUND WHEREON SHE STANDS.
BLACK, BLACK, BLACK IS THE COLOR
OF MY TRUE LOVE'S HAIR.

FAUST
She was everything I needed
or could imagine. Or rather could not
have imagined. Reality is better
than dreams sometimes, stranger. If I forgot
Barbara for an hour...If I ceased to believe
it was a kind of treason to her.
[Head in his hands, sitting at a table or desk, gun on the table—away from him.]

Life is too beautiful and terrible to grieve.

[The second record starts.]
I DREAMED I SAW JOE HILL LAST NIGHT,
ALIVE AS YOU AND ME.
SAYS I, "BUT JOE, YOU'RE TEN YEARS DEAD!"
"I NEVER DIED, " SAYS HE.
THE COPPER BOSSES
FRAMED YOU, JOE,
ON A TRUMPED-UP
MURDER CHARGE...
"TAKES MORE THAN BULLETS
TO KILL A MAN,
I NEVER DIED," SAYS HE.

FAUST
[Toward the end of the following passages he puts the gun back on the wall, goes to the window, and finally to bed.]
I cannot feel sorry for myself.
My pain is bearable. There still is work.
Even if I don't believe in anything final,
it's nonsense to think that devils lurk
behind every advance we make.
My life is dry and narrow by choice
or lazy drifting. I never act. I stake
my hope on publishing, publishing until my voice
—photocopied and blurred—is known
on every campus where scholarly pap
is chewed up by Wagners to the inky bone—
and reissued as even drier, duller crap.

FAUST (continued)

Well, Faust, that's the bed you've made.
No use complaining—it would be hard to change.
Meanwhile, have a drink, and watch the quiet fade,
watch the glare come up—note the range
and variety of life beneath your window.
Remember how many times you've meant
to get involved again, one way or the other.
But somehow life has never sent
a messenger beautiful enough or urgent enough.
So you'll go on getting angrier, more learned,
more shallow—until something calls your bluff.

[Faust turns off the lights and leaves. The record player has one more song to play before it shuts itself off, so the following song is out of the dark—except for the red pilot light of the record player.]

WHEN DAFFODILS BEGIN TO PEER—
    WITH, HEY! THE DOXY OVER THE DALE—
WHY, THEN COMES IN THE SWEET O' THE YEAR;
    FOR THE RED BLOOM REIGNS IN THE
    WINTER'S PALE.

THE WHITE SHEET BLEACHING ON THE HEDGE—
    WITH, HEY! THE SWEET BIRDS, O HOW THEY SING!—
DOTH SET MY PUGGING TOOTH ON EDGE,
    FOR A QUART OF ALE IS A DISH FOR A KING.

THE LARK, THAT TIRRA LIRRA CHANTS—
    WITH, HEY! WITH, HEY! THE THRUSH AND
    THE JAY—
ARE SUMMER SONGS FOR ME AND MY AUNTS,
    WHILE WE LIE TUMBLING IN THE HAY.

BUT SHALL I GO MOURN FOR THAT, MY DEAR?
    THE PALE MOON SHINES BY NIGHT:
AND WHEN I WANDER HERE AND THERE,
    I THEN DO MOST GO RIGHT.

[The record player snaps off and the light goes out.]

END OF SCENE 1

SCENE 2
Park Area Between the University and Town

Students on their way to town. Townspeople out for the sun.

SEVERAL STUDENTS
Why go that way?

OTHERS
We're going to Morgan's.

FIRST STUDENT
We're going to Hank's Hide It.

YOUNG TOWNSMAN
I prefer the Owls.

SECOND STUDENT
It's in a phony neighborhood.

OTHER STUDENTS
How about you, "Agnew?"

THIRD STUDENT
Come to Sweeney's. Good atmosphere,
easy broads, cheap beer.
And plenty of good arguments—

FIFTH STUDENT
So what, "De Sade"? You
always lose anyway. If your prick
is as small as your brain—you're in trouble.

WORKING GIRL
No, I'm going back to town.

SECOND GIRL
He'll be here any minute.

FIRST GIRL
It doesn't make much difference to me.
You're the one he follows like a calf.
You'll be making out in the bushes—
I'll be sitting around—don't laugh—

SECOND GIRL
He said he'd bring his curly-headed roommate
for sure, this time.

A STUDENT
Hey! Look at those two! There, don't point.
Come on. Who needs the dog-damn sun?
Draft beer, cool joints, hot broads,
(and early spring) all turn me on.

EXPENSIVELY DRESSED GIRL *[to her friend]*
Look at these boys from good families.
They could associate with the best.
Instead they're after factory girls—
with easy laughter and teasing breasts.

SECOND STUDENT *[to the first]*
Hey, not so fast! Here's two more—behind—
there in the frilly clothes.
One of them's my neighbor's cousin.
Not bad. Oh, she may tilt her nose
but I'm sure if you're patient enough—
some night you'll get to count her toes.

FIRST STUDENT
The hell with it! I don't like their walk.
Hurry up: the other two are way ahead.
That starchy type bores me with their talk.
It's something soft and kind you want in bed.

CITIZEN
Our new mayor is not good either.
When he took office it went to his head.
If anything, the services are even worse—
next time I'll vote for Winterbalm instead
of this guy who keeps changing things around!
Leave things alone. That's patriotism! That's sound!

TRAMP *[singing]*
HEY, LADIES AND GENTS, THE SEASON IS SPRING.
YOU'RE YOUNG AND HARD-WORKING
BUT I KNOW THE STING
OF AGE AND THE WINTER
THAT'S LURKING, THAT'S LURKING.
SO GIVE ME A FEW BUCKS, YOU'RE YOUNG AND RICH.
GIVING'S THE TRUE JOY—NOT JUST SMILES.
WE ALL END IN A DITCH.

ANOTHER CITIZEN
On Sundays there's nothing I enjoy
more than talking about war—from far away.
Or threats of war, or old wars,
just so they never mar my quiet day.
I like a good dry wine with friends
and to watch the boats float by.
And maybe walk around at evening
and watch the peaceful, changing sky.

THIRD CITIZEN
Yes, brother. I warmly agree.
Let them stand on their heads if they must.
Let them turn everything around—who cares?
But don't come in my yard and kick up dust.

GYPSY *[to the expensively dressed girls]*
Oh, such beautiful clothes! Such alluring young ladies!
Who could fail to respect you, to admire—
don't be afraid. I hold my tongue.
I can get you your secret desire.

FIRST YOUNG LADY
Come on, Aggie. These gypsies are for fools
without education—like my mother. I'm full
of good signs. My astrologer says
my lover will be born under The Bull.

SECOND YOUNG LADY
Mine will be connected with The Crab.
That's good—I think. Maybe a soldier or a preacher.
[she scratches herself]
But frankly, if I don't find him soon
I'll settle for anything—a writer, a teacher...

ATHLETE'S SONG *[they pass through singing]*

DEFENSEMEN ARE
STUBBORN
AND SO ARE
SOME GIRLS,
PRETENDING TO STUDY,
SHY AS THE SQUIRRELS.
BUT THEY ARE
WATCHING,
WATCHING
FOR "GRACE."
AND WE'RE
LOOKING TOO—
NOT JUST
AT THE FACE.
BOLD
IS OUR ACTION.
AND QUICK
ARE MY HANDS.
SHE'D BETTER
BE CAREFUL
BENEATH THE DARK
STANDS.
FOR AFTER
THE GAME, DEAR,

ATHLETE'S SONG (continued)

THE PLAYERS
GO HOME.
I'M TOO YOUNG
TO TAME, DEAR.
IT'S SUCH FUN
TO ROAM.

[Enter Faust and Wagner.]

FAUST

Look! New fresh life wrestles for power
with the old season's savage attacks
of cold and death. But spring sweeps over
the frozen whiteness. The sun
kisses life awake. Green will cover
the scarred fields. The first of May
frees nature and man and lets loose
their flood of love and play.

WAGNER

Dr. Faust, its a pleasure to talk to you.
I often learn something I can use.
But these pagan orgies are too strong a brew.
They're not the kind of life I'd choose.

FAUST

What you call "pagan" is animal health.
Now they worship nature and real glories:
sunlight, the sea. Summer is in the skimpy dresses,
the love-making, the raucous songs
where man desires, takes chances, longs.
It's all a hymn to the sun—to sex and birth.
"This hour," it sings—and being one with the earth.

WAGNER
Well, fornication, cursing, drinking,
are all right in their place, I suppose.
But the cultured man prefers just quiet thinking.
The low, lust-wild wretch reaps trouble—which he sows.

YOUNG PEOPLE *[dancing around a tree—girls' voices in quotes]*

THERE WAS A COUNTRY BOY WHO WENT
TO EVERY FAIR THEY EVER HELD,
ALL DRESSED UP LIKE THE DUKE OF KENT.
HURRAH! HURRAH!
"THE FIDDLE-BOW WAS PLAYING."

HE CUT IN FOR THE PRETTIEST GIRLS.
SOME ESCORTS FROWNED, AND OTHERS SNARLED.
BUT HE WAS WIDE-EYED AT THEIR—CURLS
HURRAH! HURRAH!
"BE CAREFUL WHAT YOU'RE SAYING!"

NOW 'ROUND THEY DANCED FOR HALF AN HOUR—
THE ESCORT STARTED DRINKING.
"I'LL HAVE TO LEAVE, PERHAPS TOMORROW..."
HURRAH! HURRAH!
HIS HANDS COULDN'T HELP BUT STRAYING.

SHE WAS SO VERY PRIM AND PROPER,
"NO, WE CAN'T LEAVE—EVEN FOR AN HOUR."
BUT HE ENDED UP UPON HER.
HURRAH! HURRAH!
AND THE FIDDLE-BOW WAS PLAYING.

OLD WORKMAN

[Approaching Faust from the other side and shaking his hand.]

Doctor, it's good to have you here!
We're on a picnic, as you see—
talking over cheese and sausage and beer
of the bad old days. But don't let me
ramble on too much—come have a drink.
We'll drown our losses before the sun
sneaks off. Let's talk. And let the mugs and glasses clink.
Full, fearless days to Dr. Faust—and nights of fun.

FAUST

Visions and victories to you, Norm—and your gutsy crew.
Purpose and joy in everything you do.

OLD WORKMAN

It's fitting, Doctor, that you see us happy.
There were grim years of hunger and pain.
I remember that winter 25 years ago
when your father worked months—all in vain
to prevent them changing the county law
to pull in the scabs and break our backs.
But we organized and fought back and won.
Now our own weasels crawl out of cracks.
But you're still our friend. Always we know
that Faust is one voice for our cause.
No matter what the cost to yourself
you tell the truth—and what's hidden by laws.

FAUST

[warmly, with his arm around the workman's shoulder]

It is your passion and energy we need;
without them politics is fraud and greed.

[After shaking hands and drinking with all of them, Faust and Wagner walk on.]

WAGNER
It must be a pleasure to hear such praise.
It seems they really mean it, too.
I don't think I've ever seen
the passionate respect they show to you.
A boy comes running up, "Who's that?"
His father smiles toward you and tells
about battles that you both went through.
The boy nods, turns, runs back, and yells,
"It's Gordon Faust who drove Joe McCarthy off."
His playmates gawk your way. You'd almost think
that you were John L. Lewis, or some link
they needed to the past.

FAUST
A few more steps, Wagner. To the big, belly-shaped stone.
We'll rest there, if you want. I used to come
here at midnight just to be alone
when I was active in the buzz and hum
of politics. I used to plan my work
here in the healing dark. I really thought
that we could change lives. That was a quirk
of my youth—and what my father taught.
He was, in retrospect, a naive man
who could solve any physical equation.
He knew history, too, and had a plan
for everything—except the dark invasion
of knowledge and reason by animal need.
"Need." He'd challenge that word. He'd say
I meant—human habits shaped by greed
and therefore changeable. When? Tomorrow? Today?
No, I'm sadder and older than he
could ever have been. I have no hope
that the world can be helped by me.
We can't keep down the darkness—we grope
at the mercy of our glands and childhood.
I half believe in Buddha, half in Freud.
I'm haunted by the self-deceit of "being good."

FAUST (continued)
I'm restless, empty. I fear I've toyed
with these open-hearted workmen. I helped,
my God, to build a union that's grown
both fat and racist. I think I've whelped
a wolf. I should, of course, have known
that everything changes—either slow or quick,
becomes its opposite. But deeper still, I admit
that what Norm told me is true. I should stick
to the struggle. Plant, water, weed, watch. You can't quit.
But, I'm tired. I do not believe anymore.
And without belief…no telling what's in store.

WAGNER
Why let it bother you, Doctor? You tried.
That's all a man can do. He uses
what knowledge he has and learns
a little more. He thinks, he chooses
one path—it may be wrong.
But he preaches duty, righteousness, hard work.
He adds a piece or two. The new men
will respect you—even the wildest young Turk.

FAUST
A man is lucky if he can be content
with our primitive thought and tools.
See our brutality and your heart is rent.
We're partly cavemen, partly smiling fools.
[He makes a sweeping gesture toward the view in front of them.]
But look, this view? Nature is better than thought.
A billionth of its fire is all we've caught.
[pause]
See how the sunset has the houses glowing
against the calm of green, green, green.
The light dies down, the day is flowing
back into peace. But the part we've seen
is toy-like and tame. Over the Pacific it's morning now.
From planes you can race the sun and watch
a silent world. (If only I knew how
to have that distance and yet never botch
my dreaming with too much coldness—or heat.)

FAUST (continued)

From above the mountaintops glow red,
the valleys are a sleepy brown, the most savage sleet
is pure, perfect pattern. You watch instead
the ocean, black, bristling, with its own
gorges and churning mountains. Day marries night.
Dozing, dreaming, you flee the limits of blood and bone—
Later the night deepens and from nowhere, subtle, mysterious,
the calls of free birds haunt us—part pain, part trust.
We want to cry out, "Freedom! Change!"...We hope, we soar.
Mired in routine, terror, mud, our jungle floor.

WAGNER

I've had, at times, some strange stirrings.
But never anything like those.
I soon get tired of snakes and bugs.
I become myself in fine, well-fitting clothes.
For adventure give me a good library.
You can drift from book to book, from stack to stack.
You can defy winter with dry, steady heat—
and look up anything, no risk to hold you back.
And when you find a new, small lead—
it's what heaven must be! It's all you need!

FAUST

You're a man of muffled impulses.
Never let them break loose, my friend.
I'm of two minds on every question.
I could rest if that tension would end...
Half of my being loves this life.
The other half wants out—tonight.
Partly I just want deeper roots,
partly some subtle perfume, some sensuous delight...
If I believed in devils or gods I'd pray
for them to send a sign, or bribe, or magic box
so I could "sell out" or simply stay—
huddle with the chickens or the moonlight fox.

WAGNER
I've learned to be calm and moderate.
Any persistent passion is a danger.
These days you risk your reputation, your job,
consorting with a sly, subversive stranger.
And that's only defendable and decent!
Our government knows best. I always say,
"To protect freedom means stamping out
belief in any brash, rule-breaking way."
People protest war and poverty too much.
They're pawns of some pushy left-wing bunch.
[He senses Faust's boredom and contempt.]
But let's start back. The air has changed.
I've lost the urge to browse or roam.
On nights like this you learn to value home.
[Wagner is near-sighted.]
Doctor, you're staring like a child of three.
Is it a ghost? A wild thing? Chained up or free?

FAUST
No, in the bushes, a strange dog.

WAGNER
I noticed him. A common cur.

FAUST
No, look closely. He's—unusual.

WAGNER
Just a wild, wandering dog.

FAUST
He's following us. Watch.
Half wolf, half bloodhound.

WAGNER
You're imagining things.
He's nothing special.

FAUST
I'd say his master either beats him,
or spoils him.

WAGNER
He's probably lost and planning to adopt us.

FAUST
Come here, boy. Calm down.

WAGNER
You see he's canine enough.
Stand still, he waits, and stares.
Pet him, he wags. Threaten, he grovels.

FAUST
Notice the fancy tag.

WAGNER *[reading the dog's tag]*
The dog's name is difficult to make out.
"Mada" or something close, owner "Smith, John W."

FAUST
I suppose we'll have to take him home
and call his master up.

WAGNER
He's a well-bred, costly dog.

FAUST
I prefer the unpetigreed.

WAGNER
No, breeding tells. You can breed a dog for running skill,
or gentleness, or knowing how to kill.

[They go off with the dog.]

END OF SCENE 2

SCENE 3
Faust's Study

Later the same night. This time, however, Faust is casually dressed—but not ready for bed as in the first scene. He expects a visitor. His desk is strewn with open books and loose notes. The library section of the study (1/3 to 1/2) is to the back of the stage (away from the audience). It overshadows the end of the room. There is one section of massive sets of books. But even these bear the mark of use. That is, some are not back all the way in place. A few sets show the gap where the books have been replaced above the gap horizontally. Faust is a scholar, but not a pedant like Wagner. Another section has all brightly colored and various shaped modern and paperback books. They are in some disarray. Faust is a restless man. The mid-section of the room has a picture window on one side of the long desk that runs from front to back. On the other side are works of art of some power and originality. Chief among these is a plaster copy (or a very large photograph) of Rodin's Balzac. *The door through which Smith will enter is either to the front and side of the stage or is merely imagined. In any case, Smith comes up from and goes back into the audience by way of steps to the stage. By preference Faust is of average size and shape, Wagner is short and stout, and Smith is tall. Smith is the "living result of a vast observation of the world." He is also—"Activity." But it could be argued that there is an element of restless compulsiveness about his activity—that, in spite of his immense irony, wisdom, and charm, the activity can never cease for an hour because he has no inner core or sense of peace. Smith is each of us. He is also Captain John Smith of Virginia and the Wayland Smith of English legend. He is the owner of and spokesman for the great smithy of the world where the "soul" of man is tested.*

At a large table, Faust is working hard on his new book, Jefferson of the 21st Century. *He alternately goes to the shelves to take down books, makes notes, reads aloud, etc. The dog is very restless.*

FAUST

Be quiet, mutt, settle down, lie there!
He paces and paws at the door and snorts like a chained-up bear
reliving the chase, the cries, the gore.
I'm restless too. But I use the night
to dabble in my dry but deep delight:

FAUST (continued)

Jefferson, *Jefferson of the 21st Century*!

[He thumbs through his manuscript until he comes to a passage which he reads aloud.]

> "When this government was first established, it was possible to have kept it going on true principles, but the contracted, English, half-lettered ideas of Hamilton destroyed that hope in the bud. We can pay his debts in 15 years but we can never get rid of his financial system. It mortifies me to be strengthening principles which I deem radically vicious, but this vice is entailed on us by the first error."

The first error, cur. Do you hear?
Of course, he's so young and innocent he means
Hamilton's hard-hearted error—not God's.
He's full of the simplicity that cleans
our gory face and hands and only sees
a world made bright by struggle and reason.
He doesn't believe in jungle but in Virginia trees:
consolation, shelter, fuel—each in their season.
Hell, boy, this is tomorrow's man.
I have to believe it. And sometimes I can.

[Again he thumbs through the manuscript until he comes to another passage.]

The irony is, he's writing to Dupont.

> "This is, perhaps, the only moment in your life in which you can acquire that knowledge. And to do it most effectually, you must be absolutely incognito, you must ferret the people out of their hovels as I have done, look into their kettles, eat their bread, loll on their beds under pretense of resting yourself, but in fact, to find if they are soft. You will feel a sublime pleasure in the course of this investigation, and a sublimer one hereafter, when you shall be able to apply your knowledge to softening their beds..."

Today the "liberal" mocks at that.
He's not even content with words *plus* acts
from radicals. No, *you* must strip off every trace of fat
or you're a hypocrite. Meanwhile *he* stacks

FAUST (continued)
up piles of expensive junk and never does
one lie-smashing deed to hurt the owner's feelings.
Pompous horseflies who swoop and buzz,
piggish "house slaves" who live off massah's peelings.

Stop howling, hound. Your master's on his way.
Your fur is rising as if you sense
some struggle—or smell some prey.
There's nothing to fear, cur—no clouds so dense
with danger and death as those we imagine. Yet
I envy you: all energy, all panting life.

[There is a knocking at the door and Faust opens it.]

FAUST
Mr. Smith?

SMITH
The one and many. I take a lot of kidding.

FAUST
It's a good, solid name.

SMITH
Old. Old and common as mushrooms.
You're Dr. Faust?

FAUST
Child of legend, father of questions. Yes.

[They walk into the room.]

Your dog's been restless.
He's like a gypsy in jail.

SMITH
We travel a lot. I'm pleased and obligated
that you brought him home.

FAUST
It was nothing. You're not from here. What business are you in?

SMITH
I'm what you might call a land hunter. I buy here, sell
there. Take my profit—sometimes losses.

FAUST
I suppose it's usually profit.

SMITH
Usually, usually. But never really enough.
Where there is a desert or a forest
I see great buildings—cities in the rough.
But it never works out completely.

FAUST
Never?

SMITH
Oh, we make money but then the mob,
the herd gets together, agitation, new laws.
They hem us in—or try to. We sell.
So there's compensation. But the constant movement gnaws.

FAUST
Why should it? Isn't your business—profit?

SMITH
I don't really need more money.
Neither do my friends. We crave—
power, I suppose. Responsibility.
To feel alive—in control—to explore the cave
of life—the world...

FAUST
We all set traps for life—
and end up caught and crippled. I've been
half-way dissatisfied with writing, teaching, thinking...

SMITH
Half dissatisfied? Oh, Doctor, if you waste
your life in academic quibbles,
when you're sixty it's ash you'll taste.
The whole wine jug of life turns vinegar.

FAUST
I suppose chambers of commerce make you welcome
once they smell the money…

SMITH
Most merchants are fools and philistines.
They don't want anything difficult or bold.
Yesterday's rut and glut is what they like.
Risk? Newness? That leaves them cold.

FAUST
Well, are politicians brash enough?
And hungry enough?

SMITH
Brash and hungry, they are indeed.
Scratch any "law and order" man—you find a crook.
Slippery, stupid, swollen up with greed.
I try to keep them honest and off the hook.

FAUST
Oh, come on, Mr. Smith! Honest?

SMITH
By that I mean: within the law.

FAUST
Yes, but the worst crimes are always legal.
What if you find the law inconvenient?

SMITH
We have it changed. Laws grow obsolete.

original photo from *Daily Work*

1948: Mundt, Thomas, Stripling, McDowell, Nixon

1988: Meese, Baker, Reagan, Bush, Shultz, Weinberger

Smith: "Scratch any law and order man — you find a crook."

FAUST
My friends would say you chisel and claw
to grab at profit or power—
buying politicians, perverting law...

SMITH
I represent new ways for old opportunities.
My ancestors explored the frontier with Col. Washington,
hunting, even then, for bargains in land.

FAUST
But what of the price in human terms?

SMITH
Faust, the weak always suffer—everywhere.
Good cities let in energy and air.
I'm working on plans to make over
a third of Chicago.

FAUST
For the better? Or for the profit of speculators?

SMITH
Both, Doctor; they go together.

FAUST
Go together!

SMITH
The clever and the energetic see the future.
When I was a kid a gang of us sold
an insect spray for old super-salesman Casey.
He told us it was from a clean, new factory.
One of the older men checked out the address
and baited him at the next meeting with the facts,
"Three old biddies in the back of a dingy store."
But Casey shouted him down,

SMITH (continued)
"You fool! It's on the other corner, you fool!"
Ten years later there was a factory. And it was good—
economical and efficient.

FAUST
I don't see how that excuses anything.
I happen to know "urban renewal"
and how it guts the poor.

SMITH
Dr. Faust, let me admit, I know your work.
I've read both the books and I admire
a certain sweet naivete of tone.
It's what I lack myself. I'm too much fire.
I could use your art of hurling padded stone.

FAUST
"Hurling padded stones"?
Well, I suppose.
I don't think of what I do as art.
I strive for complete honesty, complete simplicity.

SMITH
That's the most difficult art of all.
I'm after the opposite, magic, illusion.
Faust, some night I'd like to show you my plans.

FAUST
I wouldn't mind. But I don't see....

SMITH
Someday you will. Faust, this statue?

FAUST
That's Balzac. Rodin's concept of Balzac.

SMITH *[pointing to lower half of the statue]*
My God, look at that great tool!
There! That's Balzac, all right. That's any man
of force and imagination. I never heard
of one who didn't pant and plan
after every available, marvelous bird.

FAUST
I didn't notice that. Look at the head.
It almost seems to be emerging out of stone.
Critics hated that statue—called it, "the snowman."

SMITH
Snowman, hell. It's every first-rate man. Faust,
just between us, aren't you a little..."repressed"?

FAUST
Distracted, at least. For years it's been dull, drab work.

SMITH
And tawdry, tepid affairs with faculty wives
where the old fool is so tired he pretends
not to notice? And soon neither of you care enough
to inconvenience yourselves.

FAUST
Smith, you're shrewd and earthy enough.

SMITH
Doctor, I'll let you get some sleep.

FAUST *[seeing him out]*
My God, the night is mild again. Like the first day of spring.

SMITH
When I was a student in Germany—
It seems centuries ago—

SMITH (continued)
there was a strange song…
[Smith singing]

BANISH, BANISH
ALL BLACKNESS
THAT BLINDS US.
LET THE LONG LIGHT
OF SUMMER
COME FIND US.
MAKE THE MENACING
CLOUDS CAREEN.
STARLIGHT IS SPARKLING,
SILVER ITS SHEEN.
AIR IS ALIVE
WITH MAGIC
AND YEARNING.
WIND WHISPERS—
BEARING AND BURNING:
LONGING,
LOCKED LOVERS,
FLOWER ON FLOWER.
NO CLOTH NOW COVERS
THE NIGHT'S
FIRST FRAGRANCE…
TENDERNESS TOUCHES
ON APRIL AIRS.
IN DESIRE
ALL DANCES AND DARES,
ALL RIPPLES AND RUSHES.
GRAPES NOW
ARE SWELLING,
ARE READY,
ARE TELLING
OF LONGING AND LEISURE,
OF BURSTING
OF RIVERS,
OF THIRSTING
AND PLEASURE.

SMITH **(continued) [singing]**

SWIFT, SWIFT
TO THE SWEETS,
TO SLUICES AND SPICES
WHERE MARVELS ALL MEET,
WHERE DELIGHT IS. ALL WILL ARISE
BOLDLY AND BARE,
LIGHT IN THEIR EYES,
OVER THE OCEANS
SWIFTLY BY PAIR,
THERE THEY
COME BLAZING,
AND SINGING,
AND GLOWING,
PRACTICING, PRAISING,
THE FORCE, THE FLOWING.
SOME OF THEM SCALING
SNOW PEAKS IN SECRET,
SOME OF THEM SAILING
WHERE SIRENS SAY, "SAIL"—
FEARLESS OF FAILING,
ALWAYS YEARNING AND YOUNG.
ALWAYS KINDNESS AND KISS.
ALWAYS ALL FEEDING
ON MYSTERIOUS BLISS.

FAUST
It's amazing that you should remember it.

SMITH
There are times when it seems I can never forget anything. Good night.

FAUST
Good night.
Come again.

[The scene ends with a restless Faust pacing in the doorway and looking out into the spring night.]

END OF SCENE 3

SCENE 4
Faust's Study
TWO WEEKS LATER

Smith knocks; after a few moments Faust looks out, opens the door and asks Smith to enter.

SMITH
Well, Doctor—I leave today. Twice you said no,
but not very firmly. So again I ask
you to come east with me, Faust.
We'll drive through the mountains with a flask
or two of Scotch, with our butts in contour seats,
with the sun and moon competing like two
wild Picassos. Every swooping turn
will show valleys and shadows, always shifting, always new.
It's only this way of rushing into life,
believe me, that makes it bearable and good.
This stuff here *[he gestures at Faust's room]* is weakness and withdrawal.
Its only action shows you've lived and understood.
You've passions that are deep and strong. Its clear
you're too bright not to find it boring here.

FAUST
Worse! Each dull day I'm learning
to see my life here as a living lie.
To see friends leaving, dreams turning
to ashes, sweet summers rushing by.
Are we to notice such losses? No. Deny,
repress, conform. Grow deaf to cries
of pain. "Adjust," the cowards sing.
Year by year belief and purpose dies.
At dawn I wake in anguish.
Tomorrow's rages, regrets, tears
won't bring back the lost chances
in these cautious, wasted years.

SMITH
I understand you. I think...

FAUST
If I dream of any pleasure
you can be sure it won't last.
Because my whining "conscience"
whispers warnings 'til my chance has passed.
When night comes I lie down
not to peace or simple rest.
No! Fear and guilt haunt me.
I'm pious, spineless, obsessed.

SMITH
You're too hard on yourself.

FAUST
The fever that burns within me
is hot enough to drive me wild.
But when I face the outside world
I grow as cautious as a child.
So life grows dull—a gruesome wait.
Death seems a safe and restful state.

SMITH
It can never be as bad as that.

FAUST
The fortunate ones are those who die
tasting some salty victory on their lips
before it fades, or in the arms
of tender girls before the whips
of time and habit tear their loves down.
Before the bold lover
becomes a boring clown.

SMITH
You talk darkly, Faust. But I'd guess
it's all talk. In a pinch you'd bless life. And hold on to it...

FAUST
It's true I've pulled back from suicide,
remembering old loyalties and a young love.
But I was in a haze, soft and emotional.
I've played too often that callow, romantic dove.
Now I curse every illusion
that holds us to life and its pain.
They cheat and lie and dazzle us
to forget its tortures. They fog our brain
with pride. Damn puffing pride
that deceives us and dulls all sense—
and our silly, shifting games
that leave us either exhausted or tense
with envy. Damn our "high," "immortal"
drives for fame and endless life.
And low, possessive habits that set us squirming
and showing off, "my house," "my wife."
Piss on the goad of money
that spurs us to reckless feats
and lulls us with the tangled treasures
of half-dark rooms and fragrant sheets.
I hate alcohol now for its fleeting flow,
and love for its ultimate pain.
And that fool's faith that man can grow,
that's the most vicious of lies—the most vain.

[At this point a young woman comes from the back of Faust's room, pauses briefly near them (they are still near the door) and addresses Faust.]

YOUNG WOMAN IN YELLOW
Poor, wild fool!
You've turned your back
on all the beauty of the world—
spit on it!
You've given up hope.
Like a spoiled child
you strike blindly
in despair
and rage.

YOUNG WOMAN IN YELLOW (continued)
It only takes real women, real men
working on tangible problems
to make the world bloom.
That's where life is,
and sanity.
[She goes to the windows first, stands there a few moments, then goes to the doorway, turns and looks very briefly at Faust. Then she closes the door firmly, almost slamming it.]

SMITH
He may not know it but
she's on my side too.
Like any healthy young creature
she claps for action and seeing it through.
And for pleasure. Pleasure
that makes the peacock strut
while (forgive me, Faust)
here it's all...talk and sleep and rut.

Come on, quit playing with your shallow gloom.
You nurse it like some sucking, sick, pet vulture.
Among active, lusty men there's always room
for anything human. My rich and racy culture
punctures lofty shams like "high" and "low."
They have no earthly meaning except:
We feisty ones still feel sun and snow.
You high ones mince along as if you'd stepped
in dog shit. But it's in action—out there—
that you can learn to live again
freed from this stale, self-inflicted terror,
these ivory tower twinges of gassy pain.
Christ, I'd serve as guide to help you choose
among the joys of women, adventure, booze.

FAUST
But why do you want to take *me*?

SMITH
Why not? Don't worry about that.

FAUST
No, you're a businessman
and always have reasons. I think
it's better that we understand
each other before quarrels sink
the friendship—

SMITH
First, I like the challenge of your mind.
Later, if I can change it, I want you
to admit it and not go hide
behind "reputation," "consistent point of view."

FAUST
Reputation! Consistency! That garbage!
No, Smith, I'm a man of the world.
I live in my own body and feel
my own anguishes and joys. I've never curled
up for any loose tongue or fancy deal.
They can say what they want, chatter, nag.
I don't give a damn, I don't even care
if every learned committee in the States
considers me uncouth, unfair.
Reputation! Our intellectuals being what they are,
why, up is down, brutal is tender, near is far.

SMITH
Yes, you see clearly enough
what pedants and institutions always become.
I'll show you the joys of freedom.
When everything is dared—no sense is numb.

FAUST
Smith, it is not likely you can change me.
What can you offer I haven't had?

FAUST (continued)
Is there a well-loved food that never
turns cloying when you've had enough? Or a fad
in the handling of money so clever
you can both enjoy it and survive?
Or any struggle that can finally, deeply matter?
Is any woman, tender, sensitive, alive
immune to pseudo-saints who coo and flatter?
The highest honor's just a swelling bubble.
Like the hotter joys it will either pop
or drift away. I know too well that nothing
will ever last — nothing we love.

SMITH
Out there are food and games and women
to enjoy. But not to possess.
Learn that trick and you have peace.
Resist it and your life grows less and less.

FAUST
Peace is what I've never had.
Inaction yes, stagnation indeed.
If selfish activity can teach
sweet dreams while nations bleed,
well then, I'm lost to myself and won
to you. But to grow that coarse
is not my taste in perversion
or idea of fun.

SMITH
Do you have something better here?

FAUST
I won't lie. I won't say yes. But if I ever say,
this moment, this single moment is so fine
I do not care that our savage bombers
burn villages and children—they are not mine.
Or if I even say, I'm satisfied,
I wish right now that time could stop...
then, you've won me over, Smith. I'll admit it.
I'll serve and simper as your faithful fop.

SMITH
It's only respect I want. Quiet acceptance.

FAUST
It's time to take chances, to leave.
I need a man like you as guide.
Out here it's all palms and sunshine.
It's too easy to drift with every tide.
I played at Zen and dropped it,
scraped the surface of science—and turned away.
I've lost my father's belief in man.
What's left is chalk and shaping lumpy clay
unless your full-blooded bawdiness gives meaning.
Yes, Smith, let's test the limit
of rushing into life like men
who don't fear power, or death, or gods.
Or beg of brutal chance a why or when.
It's better to take the bumps and stabs
of life the way they come, without complaint,
than preen, and plan, and peek down halls
dark with loneliness and the peeling paint
of yesterday's regrets. Its movement keeps us young—
and variety for the belly and the tongue.

SMITH
There's time enough for everything.
We could be in Naples—next week.
But you can fly off, swim
in Michigan, pursue some freckled cheek
or magic thigh where lights are dim...

FAUST
It's not simply joy or women I want!
It's the whole whirling basket. The pain
at the heart of pleasure. The dark love
that's part of rage and passionate disdain.
My life is gray and gutless. It's all been above
the nose and inside my head. But now

FAUST (continued)
I want all suffering and all bliss,
everything mankind endures no matter how
savage, wild, holy. I must not miss
a drop of it—scalding tears, blood, poisoned wine...
And to delve, dredge, suffer with saints and swine.

SMITH
Faust, listen to a man who knows:
No matter how you reach and run
and rant, you can never
be part of all the jumble and the quiet.
There is no time, nor fulcrum, nor lever—
except for some mythic cosmic force
that by "definition" "understands and means."
For we stable ones it's what we can of simple pleasure.
For you? The pinch of pain, perhaps, that somehow cleans?`

FAUST
But I hunger for, I need—everything human.
Everything.

SMITH
An interesting but naive reply.
Made impossible by time, black, galloping Time.
He's kicking cinders in your blinking eye
and leaving neither reason, purpose, rhyme...
You could go grab some third-rate poet.
He'd parade you out his prissy dreams
where peace lies down with struggle and death with life—
where moonlight ecstasies don't scuttle, slow elaborate schemes.
He'll pretend one poor human can combine
self-saving cunning with self-giving love
and that all pain on this sickly planet
is part of some vibrant glory up above.
To find "affirming," praise-singing asses isn't hard.
But they're all loud-mouth liars
full of gassy platitudes and lard.

FAUST
But what is the use of partial things?
If it's this, then that, accidents, chance...
what am I? Why care what striving brings?

SMITH
On the whole, my friend, you are—what you are.
Wear fluffy wigs or elevator shoes,
drive a rusty bike or a block-long car,
the earth knows you—not the mask you choose.

FAUST
I've wasted my life in study,
lived vicariously in books.
Reality was too full of dirt and bloody
from real wounds, and too complex since all the crooks
sang, "virtue, virtue." I shrank back from fear.
And kept on shrinking year by year.

SMITH
Now you're talking like a man who sees
what the world is to practical eyes.
We must arrange to catch whatever breeze
brings luck or pleasure near us—before it dies.
What is really yours to use?
Your hands and feet and head and balls.
Use 'em, waste 'em. It's yours to choose.
And there's a more subtle happiness that calls:
the satisfaction of a thousand men
working out your plans and dreams.
All their successes are yours. And when
they fail? You spawn new schemes.
But come on, let your thinking rest.
The world offers her delicious breast.
I say a man who thinks too much
is like a cow—stubborn and lean—
who haunts a valley for a weed to munch
while every hill around him's fresh and green.

FAUST
What would we do?

SMITH
Get out of here!
This cocoon for fat, slow things
where sulking and stifled yourself, you only steer
your students toward the nothingness that clings
to random scholars. Leave with me.
Why waste your life and theirs?
If you should accidentally pluck the tired tree
of anything too deeply true, the school just tears
[Smith looks through the window at a student approaching Faust's door. Then Faust also looks out.]
your contract up. There's a student now.

FAUST
I don't know him and haven't the gall to face him.

SMITH
He looks so eager.
I'll borrow your pipe and smoking jacket.
[There should be some stage business here while Smith crunches himself down into Faust's smoking jacket, etc.]
While you get dressed I'll stuff him
with all my wisdom in a hobo packet
and done up brown. Fifteen minutes, Faust.
You get ready. I'll feed this fresh-faced monkey.

SMITH
[to Faust, who has not left the room yet, behind his back]
Just quit believing in science and reason.
They tie you to the earth, "man," "truth." Take off
with flights of faith or magic instead.
You'll be cool and clever—at talk of morals, you'll cough.
I'll keep you on my payroll 'til you're dead.
[*about Faust, who has now left the room*]
Chance gave him such a curious nature;

SMITH (continued)
he's longing for what he can't express.
Not satisfied with anything the earth can feature,
he's open to every sickness of excess.
I'll take him on a world tour of power:
starting in pleasure, getting more corrupt.
I'll show him the canker in each flower,
the hate in love waiting to erupt.
He'll come to see that coldness saves,
manipulation's all that life can teach.
The world saver—he'll see—is an ass who raves.
He'll help me keep our interests out of reach.
[*The student enters.*]

STUDENT
I'm new here, sir, but I've already
heard you're a steady, successful man.
I need the influence of someone solid
to help me discover, then execute, my plan.

SMITH
I'm a man like other men, you'll find.
I smile to see you take me so seriously.
There are good counselors here, some intelligent, others kind.

STUDENT
It's you I must talk to and trust.
I try to be both practical and idealistic,
not think only of money like my father.
But my mother says I didn't need to come.
I'd get wise enough at home—with much less bother.

SMITH
No, this is the very place for you.

STUDENT
But already I long to get away.
The campus is green, but too well trimmed.

STUDENT (continued)
You can't disturb their precious grass and gravel.
The lecture halls are always either dimmed
for boring movies, or bright and full of babble.
The classrooms are a place to sleep.
They teach everything here—but nothing deep.

SMITH
The novice needs caution and fear.
The baby doesn't grab the breast
until he's learned a taste for milk.
Then he's all bawling, eager, zest.
You'll learn to love their milky wisdom here
—better than the world's pungent beer.

STUDENT
I'd love to feast my mind and ears and eyes.
Convince me how it's not all flatness, dullness, lies.

SMITH
First, tell me which field you mean to skim.
I'll tell you if the picking's rich or slim.

STUDENT
I'd like to know the fundamental laws
of nature, and history, and art.
And then the strengths, and any subtle flaws
of human societies, or the personal, secret heart.

SMITH *[aside]*
This is the room if "everything" you blurt.
Faust is strong for lifting every skirt.

STUDENT
I'd study hard to make it possible.
I wouldn't waste much time. But I admit
in summer I like to hike or camp
or dream, or drift about, or just sit.

SMITH
Play out your green time well—it's short.
But organization will help you stretch
life out on its rack. Avoid any sort
of earthy subject. Study metaphysics and logic. Etch
their precepts in your jungle mind
until you're smooth-brained, tame, shallow, quiet,
deaf to whippoorwills—any noises you'd find
in heads unbroken to discipline and near to riot
because no heavy scholar has taken them in hand
to pimp and pander for the mean and bland.
In classes "logic" fakes names for every fraction
of a process. Freezes it for storage
in the smallest mind. The subtlest, richest action
—hear them describe it—it's a lumpy porridge,
stale and tasteless. Outside the web of motion
is as raucous and shifting as the seasons.
Thought and feeling boil like the ocean
driven by gales deeper, darker than the reasons
that shy chroniclers dare face. For what is hidden
is always the root, the "mystery," the forbidden.
Push on a bit and the "philosophers" step in.
They tease, and talk, and twiddle, and nod.
They show you why and how beneath the din
of chaos there's a "pattern"—or their newest pet name for "God."
They turn out students smug and careful as a tailor
and convince 'em they're a born, bold sailor.
"Queen of the Humanities," they've named it
—these eunuch courtiers. Always they have shamed it.

STUDENT
I didn't quite grasp all that.

SMITH
You'll get better as you learn to try
to reduce things: to squeeze out juices
and pin up skins all classified and dry.

STUDENT
I'm dazed by what you've said.
Rusty wheels start turning in my head.

SMITH
You could specialize in "THE NEW RELIGIONS."
It's the old brew, sugared, disguised—
same old function: setting up as pigeons
the weak, the unlucky, by pointing to the skies
and urging, "Love! Fly up! Love!" while the rich
continue to gut 'em, roll 'em in the ditch.
But above all, keep the rules.
Be neat, be courteous, be grave.
Instructors may be proverb-quoting fools,
your job is only to behave.
Don't question, don't press too much for meaning.
He's got a certificate that says he's ready
to teach. His mind may only be on preening,
or his elaborate house, or his steady
climb up the bug-heavy academic vine.
You must swallow grape juice, pay for wine.

STUDENT
I know. The best students are resented
by the worst teachers. You try to trim
your answers to arguments he presented.
Probing or passionate questions are threats to him.

SMITH
But you must choose a department.

STUDENT
I don't think I could stand *law*.

SMITH
Your thoughts are fresh—your feelings are fine.
Knowing the subject—from inside—one admits
they've spun a perfect spider's web for stealing

SMITH (continued)
the life out of any living thing that hits.
Worse yet, they tie their webs together, rub hands and wait—
every single human action serves as bait.
They convert compassion to folly, kindness to fraud.
When silver-haired and senile, some sprout robes and prate
of "hallowed precedents"—toadys and lunatics applaud.
Deep justice is one thing they fear and hate.

STUDENT
My doubts are made definite by you.
Your students have a chance to change and grow.
Does psychiatry dig down to what is true?

SMITH
Don't get sentimental about that shadow science.
It's full of circular arguments and proves
authority and mysticism keep their alliance
to block any bold or honest moves.
A Freudian says his patient dreams—
just what the master forecast. Adler's man agrees,
and Jung's. But each one means to opposite schemes,
and dreams and masters. Be honest—you're adrift in muddy seas.
So if you want to keep your conscience clear—
cock your head toward one and stuff the other ear.

STUDENT
Yet behind words there must be some substance, some truth.

SMITH
Truth? Behind words? Oh, be careful as a mouse.
Just when the evidence and thought get weakest, a flood
of abstract Latin nouns will try to douse
all reason with their gray but sacred mud.
Long words are a slick substitute for thought.
Preachers, politicians, swindlers—but I'm redundant—
all twist 'em daily and are seldom caught.

STUDENT
I'm sorry to ask so many questions.
One final answer—then I'll leave.
From what you've said there's only medicine.
That's not a mockery or a cause to grieve.
I've thought of it. But, my God, eight years!
And then the drudgery and wrangling starts.
What of the pain, the dying patient's fears...?
Could I take the bitter part?

SMITH *[aside]*
I'm tired of this caution. I think I'll give
the kid some pregnant hints on how to live.
[to the student]
Yes, medicine. The path is tough—then easy.
You study convoluted things. They make you sweat.
You probe and cut. And if your stomach's queasy
you puke. *Then* you graduate, relax, forget.
No more need to burn the midnight oil.
You're a white-coated businessman, my son.
Specialize in gout. Or in the boil
on rich behinds. Money equals fun.
You're good-looking—better yet.
Soon time will make you easy and more bold.
Self-confidence will teach you not to fret
no matter what you see or what you're told.
Learn to handle women with ease.
You can be certain that all you face
in their vague aches and silent pleas
leads you to one treatment and one place.
If you're half way discreet
they'll be trusting and relaxed.
They don't expect a bungler or clay feet
—you're a doctor. Now your skill is taxed.
Get off her blouse and graze her breast.
Take her pulse but hold her eyes.
Be sympathetic yet steady—that's best.
But the only winner is one who tries.
With a burning, sidelong, subtle glance
help her to sweetly slip off her pants.

STUDENT
Now the years of study have a meaning!

SMITH
My young friend, theory is dry and gray.
But life is sweet and glad on any day.

STUDENT
Your wisdom's like a dream to me.
may I come again to talk—to listen?
I'm like a caged-up child learning how to see.

SMITH
Perhaps. I'm pleased to polish my blade—to see it glisten.

STUDENT
It's difficult to leave. Before I go
assign me something tangible to study.
A quotation to remind me of this hour's glow.

SMITH
Of course.
[He writes rapidly on a sheet of white paper.]

STUDENT *[reading]*
Eritis sicuit Deus, scientes, bonum et malum.

SMITH
You shall be as God, knowing good and evil.

STUDENT
Thank you. Thank you.
[He leaves.]

SMITH
Poor chump, that blessing is a curse.
So much wiser than the animals—and so much worse.
[Faust enters dressed in a colorful leisure suit.]

FAUST
Which route do we take?

SMITH
Whichever route you choose.
But starting with the common life is best.
Then on to seats of power, money, news.
No boredom on this long and lusty quest.

FAUST
In these clothes I feel like a fool.
In crowds I've never been at ease.
I try to act assured and slightly cool;
inside I'm either boiling or about to freeze.
I probably lack the temperament for joy.
In things where you're a man, I'm just a boy.

SMITH
Faust, relax, don't care so much. See men as toys.
That's the amiable contempt called poise.

FAUST
I suppose your car is large.
To float the bumps and chase the last mirage.

SMITH
I don't go for size or show.
It's appropriateness I love.
Up in the hills I want the wind to blow
direct against me while the stars above
move cold and glittering. Down on the plains
enclosed in tinted glass, we'll drive
immune to dust, and dullness, and their boring rains.
Welcome to what's risky and alive.

END OF SCENE 4

SCENE 5

Chicago: Woodlawn Tap (Jimmy's)

A UNIVERSITY OF CHICAGO STUDENT BAR

Dan is tall and scholarly. Guy is fat and Falstaffian, Paul is "wispy." Mike is an actor, an entertainer, a wit.

GUY
No one laughing? No real drinking?
You rubes are usually rolling in the aisles
to corny drunken jokes, not sitting, thinking
like pensive philosophers with piles.

MIKE *[a little drunkenly]*
You're to blame. You usually lead
the mockery. It's your half wit we need.

GUY
[Imitating perfectly Mike's every tone and gesture, then following him around continuing the imitation.]
You're to blame. You usually lead
the mockery. It's your half wit we need.

MIKE
[After awhile, disgustedly, but with feigned anger.]
You slob.

PAUL
Whoever hits the first blow is out.
Let's sing a good old song and loud.
[*singing*]
AMAZING GRACE. AMAZING GRACE.

DAN
Whoa! You bellow like a sex-hungry bull.
But it's only our sense of hearing that you kill.

PAUL
When you can feel the glasses quake
life's all music, noise—your blood's awake.

GUY
Right. Right. Whoever takes offense is out.
[singing]
DO. DO. DO. DO.

DAN *[singing, with handout gesture]*
DOUGH. DOUGH. DOUGH. DOUGH.

GUY
Your voices are tuned. Let's go.
[singing]
THE GOOD OLD COUNCIL OF THE ARTS
IS RULED BY FIFTY ANCIENT FARTS.

MIKE *[ironically]*
An ungrateful song. A political song.
A crude song. You just be thankful
that there is a council. It's always wrong
to sneer at people who have a bank full
of money—just because they make
a mistake or six. Or sanctimoniously give
a whole sack full to a spunkless fake.
They'll soon snatch more from taxes. So if you live
an up-up bourgeois life the time may come
you'll get to squeeze their green joy with your thumb.
[He gestures.]

GUY *[singing—while staring steadily at Paul]*
SOAR UP, YOU PRETTY PIGEONS, SOAR.
TELL MY SWEETHEART UNLATCH HER DOOR.

PAUL
No, that's mush. Cut it out.

GUY
A song and a kiss for her. You can't stop it.
[*singing*]

LEAVE THE KEY BENEATH THE MAT,
LEAVE A NIGHT-LIGHT IN THE HALL.
I'LL BE QUIET AS A CAT...

PAUL
Go on, laugh. Act like a fool.
I'll wait. My time will come to gloat.
She'll leave you for some ugly, rutting goat.
Her lovers should be old gigolos
courting money, and counting up their scores.
Old belching, players of accordions or piccolos
working smelly dives for worn-out whores.
A real man is wasted in her bed.
She's not worth a copper dime.
I'd like to smash her windows instead
of crawling through them. But it's called a crime.

MIKE
[horseplay and pushing of each other half-serious at this point]
Quiet. Quiet, you characters. Can't you see
we've two lovers here. It's only fair
we twang a tune on which they'll both agree
and that will either further fog or clear the air.
Get ready and when we reach the chorus
blend in your beery basses—on cue.
Let's hit it hard until we grow half-hoarse.
What else befits this brawling, bouncing zoo?
[singing]

THERE WAS A RAT WHO RULED AND STRUTTED
IN A DAMP AND DARK OLD CELLAR
'TIL HE GREW AS DIRTY AND GLUTTED
AND TOUGH AS NELSON ROCKEFELLER.
THE COOK LAID POISON CUNNINGLY
AND THEN AS SORE OPPRESSED WAS HE
AS IF HE'D LOVE IN HIS BOSOM.

CHORUS *[shouted]*

AS IF HE'D LOVE IN HIS BOSOM.

MIKE *[singing]*

HE RAN AROUND, HE RAN ABOUT,
HIS THIRST IN PUDDLES LAVING;
HE GNAWED AND SCRATCHED THE HOUSE THROUGHOUT
BUT NOTHING CURED HIS RAVING.
HE'D JUMP, AND PANT, AND WHEEZE, AND PUFF,
BUT SOON THE POOR BEAST HAD ENOUGH
AS IF HE'D LOVE IN HIS BOSOM.

CHORUS *[singing]*

AS IF HE'D LOVE IN HIS BOSOM.

MIKE *[singing]*

AT LAST IN FEAR, BY LIGHT OF DAY
HE RAN INTO THE KITCHEN.
FELL ON THE STOVE AND SQUIRMED AWAY
IN QUICK CONVULSIONS TWITCHIN'.
THEN LAUGHED THE MURDERESS IN HER GLEE
"HE'S GASPING, GLAZED, AND GONE," SAID SHE,
"AS IF HE'D LOVE IN HIS BOSOM."

CHORUS *[singing]*

AS IF HE'D LOVE IN HIS BOSOM.

PAUL

Some song. You boobs believe it's funny
to laugh about the agony of animals
when some broad laces arsenic in their honey?

MIKE

Animals! You'd think the rat was a pet.

DAN

Poor, clumsy ox. His bad luck forces him to see
his own crazed carcass in the rat.

DAN [continued]
But that could be a lesson for you or me.
From brazen, blind gluttony we come to that.
[Lights go to Faust and Smith ,who have come in earlier.]

SMITH *[to Faust]*
Out from the chill, I bring you here
to remind you how life can be all play
when friends enjoy each other and the springtime beer.
To them, for now, each day's a holiday.
Without work and with all time to kill,
they zoom around in magic, drunken folly
like puppies tumbling down some summer hill,
—One plays the snippy terrier, one bulldog, one prancing collie.
They don't have a single whiff of worry
unless some creditor gets in a hurry.
[rising and clapping loudly]
Talent, energy, almost genius. You guys
are vintage Chicago—bitter, wise...

GUY
Thank you, thank you, Governor. And you, it seems,
are California itself: suntanned, expensive schemes,
handsome, unreal, boiling, cold—
What latest thing has Ronald Fagin-Reagan sold
that isn't his?

SMITH
Actors, redwoods, the hungry, the sick—
he's too easy and bloated a boar to beat
for such as us—for others too slick.
But you should make your acts complete.
Each can do what he wills enough.
Let go! With drink and friends the stuff
of secret dreams should sing and strut. Take 20 years.
Where will ya be then, my buckos? A round of beers.

GUY
We're Chicago guys, all right, and we don't need
encouragement from expensive dudes who think
this burgh is still half corn, half clumps of weed.

SMITH
Why, no. We're straight from Spain and even there
the people know and often comment on
how pure and quiet is your soft, safe, air.
How sound you sleep. How no mayor would piss or vomit on...
[He sings.]

THERE WAS A MAYOR ONCE REIGNING
WHO HAD A BIG PIG FLEA,
AND LOVED HIM PAST EXPLAINING
AS IF HIS SON WERE HE.
HE CALLED HIS RIPPERS AND STITCHERS.
THE CAP'NS CAME STRAIGHTAWAY.
SAYS, "MEASURE MY BOY FOR BREECHES,
AND MEASURE HIS COAT, I SAY."

MIKE
We've got the "mare" and almost fifty fleas
and crooks and clowns all heaped up in a hill.
Mount him hard, you wild singing bull!

SMITH *[singing]*

IN SILK AND BLUE SERGE GLEAMING
HE WAS NOW WHOLLY DRESSED,
HAD A COAT WITH RIBBONS STREAMING,
"STATES ATTORNEY" 'CROSS HIS BREAST.
HE HAD THE FIRST OF STATIONS,
A STAR, AND AN IRISH NAME.
SO EVERY HOOD'S RELATIONS
GREAT LORDS AT COURT BECAME.
THE BLACK AND POOR WERE MOCKED AND SMASHED,
WERE HOUNDED 'TIL THEY BLED.
FRED HAMPTON FELL, ILLUSIONS CRASHED.
OUR FLEA HAD A SWELLING HEAD.

SMITH **(continued)** [*singing*]

THE MACHINE AND MOB SAID HE HAD NO PEER-O.
THEY THOUGHT HE'D SUCK US DRY,
THEN SLAUGHTER LIKE ADOLPH HIS HERO.
WE FLICKED HIM BACK TO THE STY.

[this last line with the double gesture of flicking lice from the body and flicking the lever of a voting machine]

CHORUS *[jubilantly]*

WE FLICKED HIM BACK TO THE STY.

SMITH

What about yer dreams, my hearties?
Will ya ever do anything real?

PAUL

Guy, you'll be Dylan Thomas and a half.
Come on, sing us awake. Puff up a draft.

GUY *[declaims]*

"Star ship of fate I, float
in your bright plastic bowels. I rage
at nature and the fiends that gloat
to flesh and blood my beasty cage..."

VARIOUS VOICES

Bravo!
Murder the bum!
Get him laid!

PAUL

Stop him, he'll go on forever.
[*spoken sarcastically*]
Mike—smiling, sarcastic, clever...

MIKE
Acting and what's behind it
I mean to master. To use
our life directly as I find it.
Make fables, make ladies, make news.
You yourself, Paul, always doomed to bleed,
what special spices do you think you need?

PAUL
I plan to mix Wilder and Brecht.
Adrenaline to one, sweet up the other.
Broadway if my finger's pointing correct.
I'll get there. Oh, mother, mother, mother.

MIKE
But you, Dan, so quiet and so wise.
What sight could satisfy your Druid eyes?

DAN
All I want is mankind free,
which means the revolution growing
and sheltering like a living tree
from every doubt, hunger, storm...

PAUL
Oh, bullshit, it's applause and love,
if we're lucky, that keeps the body warm.
That's what we require and we disguise
with "ideas," and "sacrifice," and windy lies.

GUY
Well, pointing to bullshit, Paul,
your sugaring of Brecht is more than I can stand.
Your stories lack the tasty pinch of gall,
and breath and brains, and perhaps a gland.

MIKE

Guy, don't start swinging so soon.
You're like a spoiled kid at times
with a genius for beating out the tune
of self-indulgence in long, catchy rhymes.

GUY

And you, my friend, can capture
any liar's tricks, any faker's flaws.
These dolts all roll around in rapture.
But you don't search for origin or cause.

SMITH *[singing]*

THE CAUSE, THE CAUSE NO ONE CAN SAY.
JUST USE BOTH HEADS THE GOOD OLD WAY.
THE GRAPES ARE JUICY, THE VINES ARE GOOD.
THE SWEET WORLD SMELLS THE WAY IT SHOULD.
FORGET "DON'T" AND "CAN'T," THEN CHEER
FOR WHISKY, OR WINE, OR FOAMY BEER.

Live and let go and life comes free.

DAN

He's just using us. Can't you see
he's some sort of adventurer or rich collector
getting us to talk out our hopes
so he can lay some personal specter.

PAUL

I suppose he's from the FBI.
That's your "personal specter," Dan, old boy.
You radicals are all suspicious and timid.
Listening to your line we'd have no joy.

MIKE

For Christ's sake, Paul, cool down.
We were high and happy 'til now.
Come on, you be straight man, I'm the clown.

PAUL
High and happy, Hell! You guys were mocking me.
He brought magic in. He made the subject dreams.
You're all afraid to let go and really see
what's possible. You grab for grubby schemes.

GUY
Dreams! Shit, man. I hope some day
you grow up enough to admit to pain
and suffering more real than your jackass bray
against the latest broad on whom you've lain.

PAUL
Fat boy, you should talk of pain.
You baby yourself and hide from life.
[turning to Mike]
And you, my brash buffoon—avoid the rain;
it'll rust your quivering, quick knife....

[quarrelsome bickering and real anger and shoving]

FAUST *[to Smith]*
If anything could have reminded me
how glorious it *seems* to be free and young,
and how empty and tortured it really is
to be so artless, and green, and tightly strung,
this famous, happy tavern was the place.
Come on. There are memories I don't want to face.

[Faust and Smith leave]

MIKE
What happened? Why did we play the fool,
then act like animals to amuse
two strangers?

GUY
In getting us to dream and drool
of money and easy fame he turned the booze
to something beneath us and demeaning.
But it was fun to do some harmless preening...

PAUL
Nuts! He tried to show us how to live.
By not thinking. Not ever saying, "I may fail."
But by taking what's there—if we only give
our secret wishes reign—seize the world's tail!

MIKE
Was it dumb, destructive, or pleasant?
Were they really rotten—or two ripe old guys?

DAN
Could good things come as a casual present?

GUY
Are they jaded fools — or bold and wise?

[Paul approaches him scowling, and the argument continues.]

END OF SCENE 5

SCENE 6
Playboy Mansion

FAUST
This hollow laughter repels me. Can't men
enjoy the senses without a show
of self-conscious tittering? I'd prefer a den
of wolf cubs squabbling in the snow.

SMITH
You've contempt for slinky smoothness, no doubt.
Yet no respect for rude men who feel direct
and, feeling, act. Who never pause or pout
or concern themselves with being "correct."

FAUST
Meaning?

SMITH
Young roustabouts and old farmers, my friend,
both live the natural life and thrive,
cheating preachers and embalmers and in the end,
leaving a leathery carcass the earth must strive
a century to break down. But don't think
you can live like them and still retain
your quaint and quirky quibbles born on ink
or your crabby "conscience" with its precious pain.

FAUST
That's cynical—but crudely true.

SMITH
Then don't complain of scrambling and striving.
This is the haven and heaven for hard success.
Here the world's well-worshiped Gods are thriving—
here's the fruit of money, power, sex.

FAUST
I thought we'd study cold craftiness, hot rages—
and the peaks and pity of life—deeply and direct.

SMITH
If human beings careen through seven stages,
here six and three are trying to connect.
My best investments are here. I watch, I shape.
Don't credit anything but fermented grape.
[*stopping an old, pompous butler*]
Sir Salt—if you stumble on Number One, tell him
Number One-Half is here—with friend.
I'm on tour of our holdings—I have to trim.,
but never mind—my stories don't end.

SERVANT
We don't know where he is this month.
We seldom see him. He moves about.
Yet he invited all (they say) of this sprawling bunch.
Each teasing floozy, each lecherous lout.

SMITH
Don't fret, Lieutenant Lunk. I know his ways.
There was a time I tried to teach him mine.
But he preferred a more elaborate maze.
So this is what he's wove of golden twine.
No matter. We'll enjoy ourselves.
Look, Faust, you should know them,
you've seen such sports before—these flittering elves
mock every urge to love—or to condemn.

[Smith is pointing to a cluster of four of the revelers. These four should be played by same four as in the previous scene except:
where Guy was stout and Falstaffian, Monoham is all gut and gout;
where Dan was tall, thin, cool, Shocklee is bony, dried out—a skeleton;
where Mike was impish and restless, Warthog is nearly demented;
where Paul was weak, whiny and anti-feminine,
Jean Hex has become a parody of a woman.

They are all the result of what a generation of age and/or capitalism does to us. But this must be whispered to the viewer, not shouted. There is the horror—if he senses it for himself—if he hears that whisper. Faust probably half hears it.]

FAUST

They look like fools to me.

SMITH

Foolishness is judgment from outside.
You're stiff-necked and strange from within their hide.

[He addresses Monoham and Shocklee, who are bearing between them a huge silver platter.]

What carry y,e my noble struggling worthies?

MONOHAM

Caviar, my lordy lord. An' don' think
no would-be wealth-spreader goin' get it for
no beggars or untouchables—they stink.
If any tries—wif Bill and me it's war.

SHOCKLEE

Right, you tell 'em, Faddie. I din' win
no bell prize by being sof'.
I'm against *in*breeding—every sin
'cause just at the thought of *it*, I cough.
[coughs over the caviar]
War! War! War!

WARTHOG

You call me, gents? I'm there, I'm here.
An' singing for my supper.
[Grabs at the caviar with both hands—and sings.]

SAYS I, "OLD PR'S CROWDED, GEE.
BUT I'LL COME UP WITH SOMPIN' NEW,
LIKE FILMIN' SOME GRAY HORSY PEE,

WARTHOG (continued)

THEN ALL THE INTELLECTUALS WILL BLINK
AND CALL ME SHAKESPEARE—AND WE'LL WINK
AND PASS THE GREEN STUFF 'TIL WE'RE BLUE."

MONOHAM

Mr. Hogwart! This caviar is for our lovely one
who sees the future. Though I s'pose that you,
an artist, can tell which star's the rising one
so I can early change my point of view?

WARTHOG

Warthog! Ambassador, Warthog.
An' I don't give no tips
against my tender mother fog.
[He gets up.]
In fac' I tries to get back 'tween her hips.

[At this time he gallops at a window trying to throw himself out. No one pays any attention except Faust. The window is some sort of plastic so he merely bounces off, sits on the floor a few seconds, then wanders around—if anything, slightly steadier than before.]

MONOHAM *[to Jean Hex]*

Oh, Genie dear, here's Bill and me
with tiny, fishy balls for thee.

JEAN HEX

[a bony, ancient hag, acting girlish. Sitting on the floor, gaudy, dyed hair, very low-cut dress, much squirming, flirting and gesturing]
About time! Sit here to my left
and right, Mr. Skin, Mr. Bones.
[She grabs at caviar with both hands.]
These new gents are welcome too
so long as they just sits
up close beside me so they know it's true
I have some real useful tips.
[She declaims.]

JEAN HEX (continued)
[singing]

I SEE THE WORLD...ROUND
OR MAYBE FLAT

[Monoham and Shocklee nod vigorously.]

AND OUR NEXT PRESIDENT...
HE'S THINLY FAT.
ABOUT—A GABBY, GARBLED TEXT
THEY'LL BE A TERROR
THIS YEAR OR NEXT—
HERE OR OVER THERE.
ALSO OUT OF CHINA
I SMELL...NEWS.

[Monoham and Shocklee are in rapt attention, Smith aloof, Faust, looking around and getting up.]

THE BURDEN'S TOO MUCH.
THERE GOES MY FUSE!

[She sprawls backwards with arms out—meaning to be both crucified and enticing. Monoham and Shocklee fumble over her. Smith rises to follow the wandering Faust.]

FAUST
[With much movement about and puzzlement. He is in front of a large mirror-window in an elaborate frame.]

Is this trick, or picture, or the room reflected?
It shines and haunts. Calm and yet ablaze
with weavings, wishes, wonders I've neglected
while I circled in my self-centered haze.
Or is it a window to another room
where every movement goes with gentle grace?
And *she [pointing.]* in particular tears all the gloom
from within my soul forever. Now I can face
anything that age or suffering can bring
if only she be real and lives in human form.
What is the use of wisdom or power if they cling
to shriveled souls? Is she among this swarm?

SMITH
Lust and folly and their child "love" are everywhere.
So you can worry and wring hands—or take it
that she's alive and somewhere near
waiting for your worthy worship. I'd make it
ten to one you'll find your beauty soon—
and happiness as hot and endless as June.
[*He sits in a very plush armchair and swirls his cane.*]
Meantime I enjoy my power here.
I'm boss because my head is clear.

MONOHAM *[calling out to Smith or beyond]*
My lord, I think there's something wrong!
One side of Jean is flame, the other ice.

SHOCKLEE *[shaking a finger at the sky etc.]*
Mixing' brings the wrath! We won't last long!
[Monoham is pulling off her dress in haste.]

WARTHOG
[approaches, watches, and nods]
She had her place and price.

MONOHAM
[still working desperately on the dress]
She was a vision. She saw through stone.

SHOCKLEE *[keening]*
She's turning back to blood and bone.

FAUST
[still in front of the mirror-window and looking at the revelers]
Are they drunk or crazy?

SMITH *[pointing at the revelers]*
Sometimes their jabber confuses me.

MONOHAM
[holding a mirror up to Jean's nose]
I hold it up. She clouds the wrong side.

WARTHOG
She's probably croaked. I need a ride.

SHOCKLEE *[screaming]*
Death! Death! Death!
Where do I hide?

SMITH
One thing is sure:
Like animals, they're spontaneous and pure.

[A terrible hush sweeps through the room. It is Mr. Palm approaching. He is very well-dressed, except he is bare-footed. His retainers are dressed identically, except they wear low boots. As he approaches, Monoham quits fumbling with Jean and starts fawning on Palm. Jean jumps up and straightens her dress. Shocklee ceases his wailing and becomes very formal, reserved, embarrassed. Only Smith and Faust are completely unimpressed and unaffected. There are brief bars of Mephistopheles music from Gounod's Faust*; For He's a Jolly Good Fellow; Hail to the Chief; and some very beautiful and solemn hymns to the glory of God. Palm has considerable dignity, verging on stiffness.]*

PALM
You fools! One thing I forbid:
the flaunting of sex or death.
For smoothness they must be hid.
Steady your movements. Steady your breath.

[He notices Smith and Faust, both so casual and self-centered, compared to the respectful awe of his followers.]

You two! Relaxed as babies
watching, snickering, staring
as if my other guests had rabies,

PALM (continued)
or you the right to sit comparing
my place to another with a grander floor.
My associates will guide you to the door.

SMITH
[Reversing his cane, standing to his full height and smashing the chandelier.]
Guide, snide, hide.
Go fuck yourself.
Which you've often tried.
You set the tune.
I'll sing bass.
Faust will try to croon.
[Pointing the cane at Palm, half menacingly, half jokingly.]
You ass! Don't you remember the first day?
Or don't you honor any deal?
Did you think I only work and pay
while over every kingdom we could steal,
you sit ruling? You know this cane
and wallet and hard right hand,
and what was washed away or swiftly slain
to gather you this bowing, unctuous band.

PALM
My God! Pardon me. I thought
you'd always wear a beard, sunglasses, a wig.
Mystery, aloofness, was what you taught.

SMITH
This time, for old midnight's sake, I'll let it go.
It seems a century or two since we said,
"I'll see you soon." You've got the glow
of culture here. And I have read
enough in the hard book of life to fake it too.
I don't go now for noise or gaudy clothes.
I don't threaten, or curse, or bribe direct.
I choose this classic Greek Apollo nose.

SMITH (continued)
Even my walk is now accounted correct.
The heels weak for distance but you know
I've always favored the quick exploring toe.

PALM *[turning a full circle for joy]*
Now I'll have some laughs and real talk.
My robber king is back, my swooping hawk.

SMITH
Don't use that word. It's obsolete!
By robber now we mean a rough, raw, thief.
My adventures are monumental and complete.
Just call me Lord, or President, or Chief.
I'm a patron, a philanthropist. It's even said
I'm full of royal blood—that's true.
[He makes a vampire blood-sucking gesture, very quickly.]
But keep my formula in your sainted head.
[He makes the gesture of a karate chop followed by "the finger."]

PALM
Nothing you need I wouldn't give.
Our dust blew through one common sieve.

SMITH
All I want is your book of names
with little notes of weaknesses and price.
And the use of your resources including claims
on sheiks, or smilings saps, or saints who've taken your ice
and hidden it in vaults and though, "I'm wise,
all that I've done is safe from bulging eyes."
This man, my friend, needs heat and sun.
He's cooped himself with chickens who only cluck
and lay square eggs and call their quibbling fun.
He needs to know the sweetness of the muck.

[In response to this Palm makes a few executive gestures and his retainers leap into action. One bends over to allow his back to be used as a desk

where another places, and steadies, a clipboard for Palm to write on. A third produces a portable telephone for Palm to use, a fourth takes dictation, etc.]

PALM *[declaiming]*
Oscar, bring me my Walkie-Talk.
Pete, get my six sacred rings.
Rudy, dig up the flying bed.
Mabel, off the table, get the chalk;
check off everything with wings.
Fred, tell the Pope it's F & S instead.

FAUST
But all we need is a place to sleep.

PALM *[still declaiming]*
Bruce, tell number four: three weeks.
Harry, find Dick, say this:
get London Max or vanish.
Wally, six, no seven blooming cheeks.
Somebody spear me ten K fish.
Joe, now it's anything but Spanish.
[winking at Smith]
This stuff is my favorite dish.

FAUST
He acts as drunk as they are.

SMITH
He's high on power. Nothing's sweeter.
They drink to hide weakness from themselves.
His slang just jazzes up the meter.
Their mumbo jumbo's from the back of shelves
where "mystics" stash evaporated booze.
Men love authority and nonsense beyond all measure.
What they hate is earthy, tangy news.
They push away plump and pithy pleasure
to stay stoned on ancient stinking brews.

FAUST
I think they're changing.

SMITH
Changing! They hide their worship better and their woe.
But show me a doctrine where the mystic "three"
doesn't console 'em with its moonish glow.
While the secret's there—above her knee.
[He makes a little triangle gesture with thumb and first two fingers—thumb below.]

PALM *[still declaiming]*
All right. But in silver and plastic.
Photographs, passports, secret numbers.
No plot's too subtle, no scheme's too drastic.
No murder cuts a copper's slumbers.
Every code and road on cards.
No nice Nelly detains them. No law retards.

[Palm's followers have alternately been pressing in to get a view of the great man and then moving back in fear and embarrassment.]

FAUST *[of Palm's followers]*
What possible purpose, pleasure or sense?
They close in a tight and gibbering cluster,
then tumble back beady-eyed and tense.
My head aches. This noise and bluster!

SMITH
All right, Palm, you've performed and put out orders.
My friend is tired but we'll revive him soon.
He's "innocent"—which usually borders
on deliberate blindness. Lacking luck *or* the silver spoon,
men make a virtue of poor hearts that bleed.
We whisper to 'em what they really need.

PALM

[Slowly dropping in both Smith's and Faust's hands seven plastic cards—which the frantic efforts of his retainers have produced.]

These open every door. These get you in.
Even New York is sweet and tender, and old men strong
if *Palm* is with you—nothing can be sin.
Whatever you do, weasel out—and admit no wrong.

SMITH *[to Faust]*

With these gifts, that gab, he's Santa Claus or God.
I was with him when he happily trod
and manured himself a stony farm.
[to Palm]
Palm, I'll be around and one step from harm.

PALM

Call me. And remember our old song
about risk, and ripping off, and the kneeling throng.

SMITH

All I remember is that we were young.
[to Faust]
Come on, the next thing we need
is fresh air, and sun and exercise.
You're ready now to reap, then seed
—and learn again to use your hands and eyes.
There's noble indolence to enjoy, and the perfect wine
that flows when longing and the limbs entwine.

FAUST

I'm still imagining that lovely face.
I saw her. Now there's not a trace.

SMITH

Faust, don't worry. Love, love enough
and half the girls seem diamonds in the rough.
[aside] Of course, it's easier—love lust enough
and every woman has the mystic stuff.

END OF SCENE 6

SCENE 7
North Avenue Beach

Noon. The scene is bathed in light and warmth—suddenly the Garden of Eden.

FAUST
[in a bathing suit, to a young woman who passes wearing a simple dress and carrying her shoes]
Golden young lady, may we walk
along this shining beach and talk?

PEGGY
I'm not golden or a lady and I plan
to walk along in quiet—without a man.
[She leaves.]

FAUST *[tenderly]*
That young girl is glowing and unique.
I've waited and hoped a lifetime for her.
There's nothing about her vague, coy, or weak,
but that softness would cause the dead to stir.
Her lips and cheeks are spring turned flesh.
I can't get them out of my head.
Those shy, intelligent eyes have spun a mesh
I won't be free of 'til I'm dead.
There was charm in her curt little speech.
Is love and happiness within my reach ?
[To Smith, who enters from the same direction as did Peggy. Smith is very well-dressed (in gray), and has his cane.]

That's the woman I must have.
[with "tough guy" airs]

SMITH
Which one?

FAUST
That one.

SMITH
Not her. I just saw her at a rally
where "peace" was as thick and sickly sweet as honey.
They play their own games and they keep tally
in weak-kneed, wordy ways not involving money.
I can't help you much with girls like her.
There's a million others we can get to purr.

FAUST
She's over sixteen and she has to eat.

SMITH
Suddenly you're Don Juan the cynic,
with every flower waiting for your swooping hand.
There are thorns, my boy—will rush you to the clinic
and slim, sweet souls who'll rub your nose in sand.
Be realistic in whom you hope to bed.

FAUST
Now you're the pious professor who's read
and absorbed every dry parchment in his blood.
Spare me your adages and sage advice.
My soul as well as body feels the flood
of desire and dreams—I'll pay whatever price.
Or go back to scurry with the campus mice.

SMITH
Be patient. If pushed, I'll do the job.
With cash we'll wheedle in and win—if you
yearn enough to flout the morals of the mob.

FAUST
You act as if this were intricate and new.
You who offered all oceans and women to me—
Suddenly cautious before one gentle, summer sea?

SMITH
Your sophistication is very French.
Except you've missed their cardinal rule:
he who is too hurried to simply quench
his thirst plays the pale role of nature's fool.
For enjoyment's in the chase and tender lie—
winning them by wit and waiting to your will.
All the mystery and half the fun would die
if you win too quickly and just drink your fill.

FAUST
My thirst is too deep for that nonsense.

SMITH
Indeed, then no more arguing or idle talk.
It will take thought and time.
This one could not be bought
even by Croesus Mountebank in his prime.
But with a little clever cheating she'll be caught.

FAUST
Get me the chance to see her sleep.
Or something that she wears against her skin.
Just thinking that far makes my fool's blood leap—
imagine the paradise I stand to win!

SMITH
To show I understand your feeling
and that I plan to ease your pain,
I'll start right now. Before tomorrow's stars go reeling
at dawn—you'll stand where she has lain.

FAUST
I'll be with her? I'll have her?

SMITH
Not yet.
But sure as hell she has some daytime work.

SMITH (continued)
I'll arrange all details—you stay here
and dream of the unearthly joys that lurk
when you handle the little things that she holds dear.

FAUST
When?

SMITH
Soon, hours, not days.

FAUST
Get me presents for her.

SMITH
[With his cane he makes a swift, expert gesture that cuts off a flower at the stem. He puts it in his buttonhole.]
Of course, presents. When expensive I love them.
Like fresh-cut flowers with no roots or stem,
they lie of sun-drunk health—no cause to grieve.
The sly and secret goal of gifts—is to deceive.

END OF SCENE 7

SCENE 8
Peggy's and Carol's Apartment

It is early evening and the light through the window is gold, pink, etc. The apartment is small.

PEGGY *[braiding and binding her hair]*
That man who tried to pick me up was strange.
He seemed above pettiness or lust.
He looked into my eyes. That's a change.
Thoughtful? Someone you could half trust?
I hope he knew he had no right.
Usually they're neither considerate—nor bright.
[She leaves and soon after Faust and Smith enter, Smith with a passkey.]

SMITH
Come in. Be quiet.

FAUST
Leave me alone.

SMITH *[looking around before leaving]*
It's crowded with life, unlike the mansions I know.

FAUST
Sweet, poignant dusk, your light
transforms these rooms and my tortured heart.
Can this wild, insistent love ever be right?
Night and day I long—and fear to start.
Her drawings are full of life. How naive
and passionate these pamphlets and petitions.
They fight against those who use and deceive,
and profit from terror and brutal conditions...
[He sits on a couch near a small TV set, record player, and writing table.]
Here her friends argue 'til dawn
about how the weak and poor can yet be saved,
who leads the revolution, who's a hired pawn,
which faction spoke truth, what group merely raved.

FAUST(continued)

Here she has listened to music and dreamed,
thought through painful problems, worried, cried,
written pledges, and pleas out of hope that streamed
from a life where faith in man has never died.
On nights like this she must remember childhood,
her father, kid's games, afternoons of winter sun,
the terrors and wonders of that magic wood
—its hints and wild wishes before caution's begun
to break down expectations and yearnings
and toss us bleached bones and boring days.
[He approaches and looks at her bed.]
Here's the bed that's felt her lonely turnings
and tears. And brief joy—that never stays.
Here I could hold her safe and content—
exhausted, happy, and sleeping sound,
never alone again, or worried, or bent
with bitterness. Long loves are seldom found.
They're possible if we stay open and wise
and keep brushing the scales of habit from our eyes.
[He shakes his head rapidly as if to clear it.]
I'm suddenly aware. What right have I here!
What arrogance drives me? What kinds of needs?
Faust the savant lost in lust and fear?
Quaking for salvation in quicksand and weeds?
Yet how changed from an hour ago.
Then I was eager for quick pleasure to start.
Now I want summer with her, peaceful, slow.
This atmosphere, her closeness has opened my heart.
If she came here now I'd be lost.
My bluff and bragging to Smith are unreal.
His schemes are useless, for now I'm tossed
suffering and naked at her feet—learning to feel.

SMITH

[entering with a fairly large package]
Let's go. She'll be back soon.

FAUST
I'll never come here again.

SMITH
Here's the present that will be her ruin.
We'll stash it against the door and leave.
Any woman will change her tune—
they don't break the webs I weave.
One look—she won't ever give it back
and wiser, older women would agree.
They learn to know the things they lack.

FAUST
I can't. I shouldn't.

SMITH
You shouldn't!
Well, if you want it for yourself
that makes a kind of sense. But otherwise
you'd better put your lusting on the shelf—
or sneak into a nunnery where you'd be the prize
for your precious "soul" (and body) all alone.
Qualms are for cowards, the half-way grown.
[shepherding Faust toward the door, and leaving the present outside the door]
Let's go.
It's just to win the girl's good will.
No need to think or twist your face.
You look as if you had to lecture still,
not just to students but to the scowling race
of philosophers and moralists from Year One.
That's not the way you learn to relish fun.
Come on.

[Soon after they leave Peggy enters. She brings in the package and puts it down.]

PEGGY
Somehow it's far too warm in here,
and yet outside was bone-chilling cold.
I feel confusion—almost fear.
If only Carol were home and I had told
her about this strange day. I'm a nervous fool—
one minute warm—then shivering and too cool.
[She begins to sing while undressing.]

THERE WAS A KING IN THULE
FAITHFUL TO THE GRAVE,
TO WHOM HIS SWEETHEART DYING
A GOLDEN GOBLET GAVE.

HE KEPT IT NEAR HIM ALWAYS.
AT EVERY DRINKING BOUT
HIS EYES WOULD DARK AND MOISTEN.
THE CUP WOULD FLOW WITH STOUT.

WHEN HE FELT DEATH APPROACH
HE GAVE HIS SON HIS NAME,
AND SWORD, AND CROWN, AND CITIES.
THAT CUP ALONE HE'D CLAIM.

HE CALLED HIS KNIGHTS TOGETHER—
OLD FOLLOWERS, YOUNG CHIEFS
TO HIS WINDSWEPT, SANDSTONE CASTLE
WHERE THE SEA DANCED BELOW THE CLIFF.

THERE STOOD THE OLD, SICK, LOVER—
ONCE YOUNG, ONCE KING, ONCE FREE,
AND TOSSED THAT GOLDEN STRANGE-CARVED CUP
TO THE BLUE-WHITE BLAZING SEA.

AND SAT DOWN AMONG THE LOVERS,
AMONG THE DRINKERS, AMONG THE YOUNG.
HE DID NO MORE DRINKING EVER
THAT KING WHO'D BEEN SO STRONG.

PEGGY

[In moving around the room she looks at the package.]

Why, this package at the door was for me!
I didn't expect it. I don't understand.
Blue velvet and special, as a fool can see,
[She cuts herself in trying to open it.]
tied with a cutting, clasping band.
I'll open it somehow and find, I hope,
a logical reason why it was dropped
unguarded, unexpected—if I can grope
my way to unwrapping it. My heart has stopped!
It's a painting by Matisse—*The Sun and Sea.*
It looks and feels original—real.
Who would be able to give this gift to me?
It can't be bought. My friends don't steal.
[She puts it on a table against a wall.]
My God, it makes the room a paradise.
I wish it were really mine, not a mistake.
Everything's aglow. You have to shield your eyes.
Unless your soul is dead—you're shocked awake.
Rich women get these lovely things
to hang like living trophies on their walls.
We get the broken things that poverty brings:
hunger, homelessness, unheeded calls.
Songs praise the youthful and the pretty.
But money means hope or hell in every city.

END OF SCENE 8

SCENE 9
A Street

Daytime. Faust pacing.

SMITH *[entering]*
By the pangs of rejected love! By Hell and worse!
To see it and be helpless! I have to curse.

FAUST
Who's this stranger with the pinched up face?
Of the crusty, casual Smith there's not a trace.

SMITH
If I didn't think that anything was fair
I'd snap and snarl like a baited bear.

FAUST
Come on. You play the lunatic quite well,
but there's a special story you have to tell.

SMITH
That expensive painting that we gave your pigeon
is in the hands of the very Party
that conjures up chaos with their new religion
involving "service," and "sacrifice," and things so ghastly hearty
they turn a healthy stomach. It seems her roommate,
one of those righteous, spinster nags
classifies all gifts as "just rewards" or "bait."
And stamps 'em quickly with her quirky tags.
Our Matisse didn't stand a chance.
She got the story from Peggy at once,
pushed the picture back with one frigid glance,
then lectured the child like a driveling dunce,
"He wants you grateful and in his debt.
To return it would be useless. We'll show the fool.

SMITH (continued)
The tons of medicine and milk the sale will net!"
Peggy nodded, though she thought it cruel
to kick a gift horse, and that the man
who gave it had to have deep feeling.
The local chairman came—I think he ran.
Seeing the high stakes, and the hand he's dealing
he puffs up the skinny ones' worst fears.
In chorus they cluck about, "A rich man's evil try
to win an innocent"—it would bring tears
unless you note the hard glint in his eye.
He says, "We'll pirate it for the people's good.
No matter what the source, our purpose cleans it."
Poor Peggy agreed and said she understood.
He's twice the ass if he half-way means it.

FAUST
Better they should have it in their hooks
than bankers and generals, the master crooks.

SMITH
It wasn't that he didn't take time to thank 'em.
They'd note it in their paper. Or so he said.
He forgot to say how high the gift would rank 'em
or if such "purity" bought happiness in bed.
I tell you, Faust, these radicals will be our ruin.
Pious prigs! Against green, lusty jungle—they prune.

FAUST
And Peggy?

SMITH
She's very withdrawn and quiet
and thinking often of your *Sun and Sea.*
She doesn't fault their logic—but doesn't buy it.
She daily dreams, "What kind of man is he?"

FAUST
Her hurts, her hopes are like my own.
Get her another like the first.
He didn't live through that one alone.

SMITH
No, they grow on trees. What a clown I've nursed.

FAUST
Don't piddle away precious time! She's in pain.
And cultivate her other friends with charm—
or threats. Whatever will win with the least of strain.
Once she's mine I'll undo all harm.

SMITH
Of course, my friend, it's as good as done.
[Faust leaves.]

SMITH
They'd set fire to granaries, or give a lunatic a gun.
A buffoon when he's in love would pull down skies
just so his sweetheart might roll her eyes.

END OF SCENE 9

SCENE 10

Martha's Apartment

An apartment like Peggy's and Carol's, except more lavishly furnished. Martha is very florid and lively in all her talk and gestures.

MARTHA *[to herself]*
My old man left suddenly for no good reason.
If he came back I'd strangle him—I think.
It would depend on my mood—and the season.
There are times I'd want justice, times I'd wink
at anything he's done. I can't forget
the silky touch he has. But I bet
he's forgotten by now our bounding bed.
If I were sure of that I'd wish him dead.

PEGGY *[knocking on the door]*
Martha! Martha!

MARTHA
What is it, honey?

PEGGY
[rushing in with a large blue velvet package in her arms]
Another Matisse at the door for me.
A Woman Naked, in a shimmering room.
I can't describe the beauty, you have to see—
all earth and flesh tones and everything alive.
No meanness can stand near it and thrive.

MARTHA
Better not let Carol see this one.
[making the gesture of dialing a phone]
Puff, she twirls her finger, there goes your fun.

PEGGY
Just look at it.

MARTHA
You're getting the gifts you deserve.

PEGGY
I can't hang it at the foot of my bed
and enjoy the shivers it would spread.

MARTHA
Leave it here, you innocent doll.
We'll hide it, and hang it when you come.
No need to please old prissy moll—
or tangle with her temper or tough old thumb.
You slip over here any time you're free.
I'll sleep, or bite my tongue, or leave.
You can dream for hours about what you see.
You should never fear, or worry, or grieve.

PEGGY
There's a shadow on all my pleasure.
What money's buying this tempting treasure?
That taints everything. Who's at the door?

MARTHA
A tall man I haven't seen before.
Come in.

SMITH
[presenting a card and bowing deeply]
Good afternoon, sweet ladies.
I'm looking for Mrs. Martha Mangrove.

MARTHA
I'm the one.

SMITH
But who is she? You're both so fresh
and full of life. The room is rich
and yet so soft with summer, you want to stretch
and sleep. Or dance. I don't care which.

PEGGY
I'm Peggy. It's the painting, I suppose.

SMITH
Not the painting. The air and glance of you
are like the dreams men always choose
to help them go on, and up, and through.

MARTHA
What did you want?

SMITH
I'm a friend of your husband
back from Barbados, where, I'm sad to say,
he lies forever beneath that balmy bay.

MARTHA
No! Not Bob! Not dead! Not Bob! Not him!
Now the world's cold, dark, grim.

PEGGY
[throwing her arms around Martha]
Martha don't give up, don't despair about life.

SMITH
There are other things I can tell.

PEGGY
I fear deep love just because of this.
The final loss, the pain. The touch and voice you miss.

SMITH
They're always locked like lovers—pain and bliss.

MARTHA
How did he die?

SMITH
Testing out his diving gear one night
he went down laughing into the blackness alone.
Nothing after that—no sound, no sight,
no body, no hint, no blood, no bone.

MARTHA
Did he speak often of dying? Did he worry?

SMITH
Once, half-drunk, he said, "The sea will get me
in a slow strangle, or sudden flurry.
I'll have no warning, no chance to flee."

MARTHA
Did he talk of the children—or of me?

SMITH
Yes, more than twice he talked of you
and guilt—how much better he'd meant to be.
Fearing (or hoping) that he'd get his due.

PEGGY
To carry guilt is an awful strain.
Poor, sensitive man to feel such pain.

SMITH
A tender one like you should be married.

PEGGY
Not for a long time. There's so much to do.

SMITH
At least you should have a lover to caress.
Imagine each night his coming to you.
Then the tempting, the teasing, as you undress.

PEGGY
I mean to be careful and very sure.

SMITH
One thing is sure. The folly of staying "pure."

MARTHA
Please tell me the rest.

SMITH
Just five days ago in his sunlit room
he told me of dropping his profession
suddenly—overnight. He said, "Assume
you sense each morning a deadly slow recession
of freshness and fire—it was life
leaving me marooned and hollow.
I'm sorry if I hurt others—and my wife.
I heard a siren song—I had to follow."

MARTHA
I've easily forgiven him and understood.

SMITH
Then he went on, "No wonder, she took
my youth, stuck me indoors, plucked away
booze and adventure, sank the hook
of children in me four times, barely let me stay
a drone bee where she was queen.
Work had no savor. Life had no sheen."

MARTHA
The stupid ass—no one ever understood him.

SMITH
Jealous men kept him back—and bad luck.
But suddenly six years ago—off the Cape
three divers found a liner that a barge had struck
and sent down squealing like a frightened ape.
He was in charge and they salvaged all—
millions, millions in one monster haul.
He could relax, and revel, and buy the leisure
he thought held all the keys to pleasure.

MARTHA
Then he left us rich?

SMITH
When poor, he met a black girl whose fire and wit
lent him the will power and wisdom he needed.
Whose mind kept flaming what her body lit.
She never failed him and so he gave
her all he had—both sides of the grave.

MARTHA
The dirty bitch to rob his children!
He had that rotten tendency to ramble.
Secure, loved, safe, he'd sneak out to gamble.

SMITH
That shaped his life, and shades his grave. If I were you
I'd mourn him for a fairly decent time,
but never in black or too severe a blue.
You're young, hearty, bouncy, and in your prime.

MARTHA
I'll never get a guy as good as him.
He was such a yeasty, cocky clown.
He pushed pleasure up to—then over the brim.
My heaven was—any time he pulled me down.
Except for his damn chasing and love of drink.
He never took time to stop and think.

SMITH
That would have been fine if he had said,
"Martha, just because we're married doesn't mean
we'll rage or worry who gets in whose bed—
just so when I'm home the sheets are clean."
I'd marry you myself on those good terms—
and show you why my Latin lady squirms.

MARTHA
I'm afraid you're kidding, Mr. Smith.

SMITH *[aside]*
Slowly, Smith, slowly—or go stumbling.
She'll "kid" for me or say she did.
She's so simple and lusty. She'll go tumbling
over backwards at the first fake bid.
[softly to Peggy]
Honey, has your mind been opened?

PEGGY
I don't know what you mean.

SMITH
You're so unselfconscious and direct.
[loudly]
But ladies, I *must* leave.

MARTHA
What about proof that he is dead?
I'll need that for insurance and a pension.
I'd rather have him or a shred of hope instead.
But monthly income cures most kinds of tension.

SMITH
That requires two witnesses, of course.
Fortunately, I have a friend who saw him die.
We'll let duty break our black remorse
and sign papers for you saying how and why.
Tomorrow noon, unless your agony's too high.

MARTHA
Tomorrow sounds timely to me. Yes, tomorrow.

SMITH
I hope this young lady will be here too.
He's lonely in this huge, cold city.
No one matches his sensitive soul—or very few.

PEGGY
I'll seem plain to him, and at a loss for words.
SMITH
Your charm and voice out-sings melodious birds.

MARTHA
Tomorrow then, in my sunny garden out there
we'll sit and talk and feel the summer air.

END OF SCENE 10

SCENE 11
An Open-Air Restaurant Bar

Faust at a table. Smith approaches him and sits down.

FAUST
When? How soon? How goes it?

SMITH
Good as green love. I see that you're on fire.
Well, Peggy will quench what nature lit
within the week. Tomorrow, if you desire
in Martha's gracious garden—you'll meet.
As gypsy go-between she can't be beat.

FAUST
Fine. Fine as filigree.

SMITH
One thing we have to give her.

FAUST
Anything from fish to fur.

SMITH
We must scribble our signatures and say:
she's free to wed without a worry,
her husband's with the snails in Botony Bay.

FAUST
How could we be sure of that?

SMITH
Sure! Who gives a drunkard's damn?
Long before he's back we're sure to scram.

FAUST
No. Never. That's too rotten a lie for me.

SMITH
For you it's the wrong time for reform.
For twenty-odd years you fed the kids
barrels of bullshit still odorous and warm
about the latest quack answer that rids
life of darkness, disasters, fears.
You idealist lippers invented lies
ten thousand years ago. And crocodile tears.
And sour gods squinting from the skies.
Now at some useful little fib you balk.
Perhaps you only lie comfortably with chalk.

FAUST
That's sophistry—flashy and clever and false.

SMITH
Indeed. Except I know your plans.
Won't you bamboozle poor Peggy with pledges
of love as deep as canyons—and your human glands,
and as green forever—as next summer's hedges?

FAUST
From my heart, every single word.

SMITH
How touching. If soft-headed, I'd be stirred.
But is it from your heart you say, "forever,"
knowing better? From *there* that tough and wild force?
That "heart" is quite an organ—so strong and clever.

FAUST
I only know I passionately feel
such great raw pangs of tenderness, and fear
of any pain that can touch her. My senses reel
but my conscience at last is clear.
Now I'd rather hurt myself than her.
I've made it love—no matter what drive is the spur.

FAUST (continued)
You can't call this deception or a game.
Knowledge, will, feeling transform the flame.

SMITH
Flashy and deeply false. Sophistry.

FAUST
We might as well not waste time and breath.
The cynical one-sided man can never lose
an argument—except eventually to death.
He swaggers in circles that he loves to choose.
You win this time. Though what I feel is true,
the wrong thing is what I have to do.

END OF SCENE 11

SCENE 12
Martha's Garden

Faust with Peggy. Smith with Martha. Both couples walking up and down.

PEGGY
You've seen so much and think so clear,
my talk must seem common and too light.
Your kindness changes the words you hear
to make them more subtle and more bright.
There are so many fields in which I'm green.
You know good from bad—and what things deeply mean.

FAUST
Every little gesture and glance from you
makes the world human and almost new.
[He kisses and holds on to her hand.]

PEGGY
My hands are rough. I don't get much chance
for personal things. I do always try
to take time for books—and sometimes a dance.
But around us so many suffer, so many die.
[They pass out of view.]

MARTHA
You travel always, am I correct?

SMITH
Yes, my trade allows no time for rest.
In each city I just pay and collect.
[poking her in the ribs]
There's no snug soft spot I call *my* nest.

MARTHA
That's very well when one is twenty-five.
To careen from girl to girl is fun and easy.

MARTHA (continued)
At fifty you have half that kind of drive,
more delicate tastes, a stomach turning queasy—
you're content to settle down, to share, to stay alive.

SMITH
I shudder when I think of such a fate.

MARTHA
It also waits the wild and the great.

PEGGY
But, "out of sight is out of mind."
Your affection and warmth are real,
but there are many women you will find
more cultured than I who only feel.

FAUST
Don't be deceived. That "culture" and pleasant talk
is mostly sparrow's pecking on a bony stalk.

PEGGY
Why should that be?

FAUST
Their chatter has no real depth, nor range, nor heart.
Your sympathy and tenderness are water and sun
that wake and warm the tangled roots of art.
The rest is study, patience, sweating 'til it's done.

PEGGY
Think of me when you see these fragrant flowers.
I'll think of you in any stolen, quiet hours.

FAUST
Your days are difficult and long?

PEGGY
There's never enough help or time.
In a People's Clinic you see the strong
and able, crippled and unwanted, in the prime
of life. You know that something is deeply wrong.
Carol's like a mother, stubborn, firm.
Her father was mutilated when she was five
by Franco's butchers. She says the germ
of revolution is in each poor man kept alive
in body and spirit and brought to see
which class profits by oppression and wars.
So we attack the raw, inhuman misery
with love, and bandages, and fists on iron doors.
A Black Panther woman died last year—my friend.
Nursing her, I hardly ate or slept.
Yet I didn't want those months to ever end.
Her pride and passion are lessons—gifts I've kept.

FAUST
If she was like you, she was unselfish.

PEGGY
Not unselfish, just human and poor.
I raised her baby for a year.
Her husband was jailed 'til politicians were sure
the time for action was gone. My only fear
was late-night knockings—that they had come,
the hired fools in uniform, to take the child
using some dead rule or lie. My hands were numb
from washing and extra work. That was mild
compared to the numbness of the mind from worry.
But she was so tiny, and sweet, and bright,
I'd think of her wide, trusting eyes and hurry
heedless through traffic when I got off at night.

FAUST
It was an experience of deep love—and terror.

PEGGY
And drudgery, much drudgery and distress.
I kept her cradle right against my bed.
If she slept soundly, then I'd get some rest.
When she half-way cried, I'd walk the floors instead
of sleeping. Or take her in with me
to hug and soothe with nonsense words
or real sentences. I'd watch to see
which one was best. Then before the birds
were stirring I'd get up, wash, do housework,
shop, cook. There was never time to pause or think.
Each day's the same, exhaustion and sickness lurk.
How sweet sleep becomes, and simple food and drink.

MARTHA
A woman's lot is sad. There's much abuse
from bachelors who love their running loose.

SMITH
For you that should be no problem at all.
Tempt a man. He'll never say "no" or stall.

MARTHA
I mean feeling, love, settling down.
Someone special in your life.

SMITH
I only know they say the happiest clown
gets quiet when saddled with a wife.

MARTHA
Haven't you been fascinated, sleepless, lost your head?

SMITH
Yes, I've led many a treasure to many a bed.

MARTHA
I mean serious. Have you known the heart's deep ache?

SMITH
I'm always serious with women. For their own sake.

MARTHA
You don't understand.

SMITH
I'm sorry if I'm stubborn and somewhat blind.
You—I'm sure—are always flexible and kind.

FAUST
Sweet darling, when you saw me at the door,
did you think, "Somewhere we've met before?"

PEGGY
You saw me lower my eyes.

FAUST
I still can't explain that boldness.
You were new—yet expected—someone I'd recognize
anywhere. Not to speak would be stupid coldness.

PEGGY
I thought: he probably thinks I'm easy
because I'm walking casual and slow.
Even ugly men accost one, the fat, the sleazy,
the overdressed, if they think you-half way show
some possibility of "looseness." So I blamed
myself. And yet I didn't because I need
the right to loll along without being "claimed"
by any idle fool. But my heart would plead,
"He wasn't like the others—I don't think."
Now still not knowing, I tremble on some brink.

FAUST
Sweet one.

PEGGY
Wait!
[She plucks a flower and pulls off the petals one by one.]

FAUST
A little bouquet?

PEGGY
A childish game.

FAUST
What?

PEGGY
You'll laugh at me.
[She pulls out the petals and murmurs.]

FAUST
What are you murmuring?

PEGGY *[half aloud]*
He loves me, loves me not.

FAUST
You darling child!

PEGGY
Loves me—not—loves me—not—
[plucking the last leaf, with great joy]
He loves me.

FAUST
My innocent, let that chance result
forecast fates and forces we can't see.
He loves you. That's the deepest thing he's felt.
[He grasps both her hands.]

PEGGY
My breath is taken.

FAUST
Don't fear anything now or ever.
Let these warm hands hold yours and pledge
that nothing, nothing can come to sever
what we will have between us. Or ever hedge
our love with limits—so petty, so galling.
This will last our lifetime or nothing matters
and despair tears every tenderness to tatters.
[Peggy breaks free and runs up the path.
He hesitates a moment, then follows.]

MARTHA
The night is falling.

SMITH
Yes, and we must leave.

MARTHA
I'd ask you to stay but all my neighbors
have empty lives unless they somehow weave
gossip out of nothing. Their only labor's
telling my other friends who comes and goes
and when. Their faces like their blinds are always drawn.
Their talent and their brains are in their nose.
Where's that buoyant couple gone?

SMITH
Along the garden walk they whir
like wind-tossed butterflies.

MARTHA
He's drawn to her.

SMITH
And she to him. Or else the world dies.

END OF SCENE 12

SCENE 13
A Summerhouse

Peggy enters, hides behind the door, peaks through the crack.

PEGGY
He is coming!

FAUST *[entering]*
You robin, you tease!
I've got you!
[He kisses her.]

PEGGY
[embracing him, and returning the kiss]
Dear one, I love you from my heart.

[Smith knocks.]

FAUST
Damn! Who's there?

SMITH
A friend.

FAUST
A monster.

SMITH
It's time to leave.

MARTHA *[approaching]*
Yes, it's very late.

FAUST
May I see you home?

PEGGY
Carol would…no…Goodbye.

FAUST
Can't we remain?...Goodbye.

MARTHA
Goodbye.

PEGGY
Goodbye. For now.
[Faust and Smith leave.]

PEGGY
My God, the things he knew and said.
Can one man have seen so much?
How shallow have I thought, and judged, and read.
His world is wide and glows with such
a weaving of possibilities. I can't understand why
he finds me so lovely. I won't even try.

END OF SCENE 13

SCENE 14
Forest and Cave
MISSISSIPPI PALISADES, WEST OF CHICAGO

FAUST

This earth and sky should be enough
for any man. I've lived with the awe
and anguish of animals that know the rough,
moist tongue of spring and the ancient, raw
stabs of cold and death. At times I even know
the inner secrets of process and change
like a friend's heart—and the flow
of unfolding purpose. I hear the strange
songs and cries of every creature on earth,
and feel the rush of life for room and range,
and sweet, long sleeps of summer, the blaze of birth.
When too much tension tore my heart,
when after long self-deceit I knew
I could not accept the secret, selfish part,
I found this lonely place to wrestle through
my fears about what I can't give up—or start.
Here my green storms and dreams that never stop
make each shadow loom half sensuous, half grave.
But when that yellow moon floats up
and coats each thicket with a mirage of majesty
then memories of the long past erupt
softly in my heart, and the tangled tragedy
of history weds flesh to thought and overflows my cup.
Nothing can be perfect in man.
I believe that with my blood. Desiring her,
all innocence, all life, I cannot plan
or imagine a day without the burr
of his callous cunning in my cocked-up ear.
Always he poisons love by making the blur
of subtle things too mechanical and clear,
but fans my lust while mocking it and drives

FAUST (continued)
me desperate toward her body's joy.
In all my desert thoughts that sweetness thrives.
I stride about—and brood, part God, part toy.

SMITH *[entering]*
Three days! Haven't you had enough?
How much dull quiet can you stand?
For week-end love nests I could see this stuff.
But looked at daily it's boring, common, bland.

FAUST
I wish you had something better to do
than nag me on this golden day.

SMITH
I'm wasting breath with a fool like you.
Your vapid moonings don't match your feet of clay.
You're grouchy, stubborn, defensive, blind
to your own needs and nature. I never know
what's whirling or whipping through that wild mind—
dreams of some "ideal", *or* one soft behind.
They're both fine fuel to make a fool's cheeks glow.

FAUST
At times you're too crafty and crude.
Your earthiness gets boring. You never rest.

SMITH
Poor ass! I found you dead or in a mood
for death—an old baby robin squawking at the nest.
I pushed you out to fly—a day at least
in sun. Much better than the wormy diet
of books and bookish men you choked on. That feast
of life out there is anything but quiet
or simple, or safe. So you drift back to caves
and imitate some owl, blinking, and all-wise.
There's quiet and dark enough in waiting graves.

SMITH (continued)
So most men seek soft shapes, and shining eyes.
Except you scholars, of course. You love the dead.
It's fat books and thin thoughts you take to bed.

FAUST
You can't start to guess the delights that lie
in simply watching, the peacefulness, the honey...
If you could, you'd scheme and somehow try
to make it "useful"—and subject it to money.

SMITH
Yes, blessings from nature's very heart.
To lie on mountains in the dew at dawn
and feel your soul swell up. Just as a start
you penetrate the clouds. All limits gone,
you penetrate the stars with intuition and love.
Then down, Oh, little mock-God you dive
into the mucky earth without mask or glove
to dig out anything once even half alive
and touch it with your sympathy. I'm not above
ticking off these phantoms of your "heaven" and "hell."
Need I say just *where* you really swell?
[He makes the gesture of brandishing an erect penis.]

FAUST
You idiot!

SMITH
How so? It seems I've struck a tender place.
Your heart's so pure, your love is so devout
I don't dare name the prize of all your race—
that no pure heart has ever done without.
But, of course, I don't begrudge your pleasure
in romanticizing needs. It does small harm—
in moderation. Yet already I sense this treasure
of rustic sleep is losing half its charm.
Soon once again you'll be panting, anxious, half-mad.

SMITH (continued)
One breeze will blow you bitter, the next one glad.
But that's obvious. Right now, your girl
is pining in a mood as quiet and blue
as mid-May mornings after some springtime whirl
of wind has smashed a town—all because of you.
You said you loved. You bowed and scraped—
then ran away. What's she to think
except that all was lust and only draped
in soft, silk words so you could slyly drink
the sweetness of her soul and body? It seems to me
that you should reward this tender child.
The way that all men know. Not love some tree
or landscape, however, old, or thick, or wild.
Her days are passed in singing—old songs.
What else could half-way calm a broken heart?
She laments first causes, wicked wars, crushing wrongs—
makes up in feeling what she lacks in art.
At times she cries. At other times she's sad
beyond all tears. At night she seldom sleeps.
By day she tells herself she's almost glad
your capriciousness came out. But nothing keeps
the anguish away. Silently she longs and weeps.

FAUST
Insidious!

SMITH
Do I call you home to reality?

FAUST
Don't try to deceive me. To trick me back
to smash her useful, stable life.
I may be stirred, confused, but I lack
the rottenness to spread my hollow strife.

SMITH
What will you do? She thinks your loving heart has flown.
Your head is half romantic mush, half solid bone.

FAUST
I think of her always. I can't forget
her voice, her little gestures. My longing won't end.
I could be jealous of the glasses she drinks from,
the first voices she hears, her most casual friend.

SMITH
Yes, I envy you when your lips caress
her nighttime roses freed from daytime dress.

FAUST
You play the pimp?

SMITH
Indeed. And I laugh at your scowling struggle.
God, making man and woman, saw right away
it was fitting they should entwine and snuggle
and gave near-godly rank to him who'd prompt the play.
Come back to light and life. Accept your bitter lot;
you'll have to plough with her the midnight hay,
not lie like death, hands folded—and all set to rot.

FAUST
Although I see in her my hope for joy
and know we belong together whatever comes,
I hesitate. I know I'll hurt or I'll destroy.
But life without her is dry and tasteless crumbs.
I'm a monster without plans, without deep belief,
without purpose. Like a flood of longing I've burst
in anger on the world for my own relief.
She's what I need! I'm blessed. I'm cursed.
She's everything I'm not. She's strangely free
of arrogance and shallow pride. Her life has hope
and meaning—a forecast of what could someday be.
I swoop down on her. I need. I grope.
It wasn't enough—wealth, or even fame,
the cool, beautiful women at your beck and call.
I needed youth and innocence to use and lame—

FAUST (continued)
offering my phantom glitter and my desperate gall.
Then since I must, I will. But here I swear:
though I may cause her pain I'll stay.
I'll change, however needed. I'll be for her
a help, a touchstone. I'll live the way
she wants. I'll fight restlessness and love's decay.

SMITH
Eager again, my Mr. Kid, and boiling over?
Yes, fool, go bring your respect and love.
Unless you spoiled dreamers walk in clover
you pout and brood and curse at life, or shove
and claw like some tortured, temperamental clown.
Be man enough to face brute human facts.
Don't lie, twist, sugar-coat to drive them down.
They win out anyway, not in words, but acts.

END OF SCENE 14

SCENE 15
Peggy's Apartment

She is at the window, singing.

PEGGY

TO THE QUEEN OF HEARTS
IS THE ACE OF SORROW...
HE IS HERE TODAY.
HE IS GONE TOMORROW.
YOUNG MEN ARE PLENTY
BUT SWEETHEARTS FEW.
IF MY LOVE SHOULD LEAVE ME,
WHAT SHALL I DO?

I LOVE MY FATHER,
I LOVE MY MOTHER,
I LOVE MY SISTERS,
I LOVE MY BROTHER.
I LOVE MY FRIENDS,
AND RELATIVES TOO.
I'D FORSAKE THEM ALL
AND GO WITH YOU.

SCENE 16
Martha's Garden

Faust and Peggy enter.

PEGGY
Tell me, Gordon—

FAUST
If I can.

PEGGY
About your politics, your deepest belief.
You're kind, intelligent, very wise...
But without class insight—we head for grief.

FAUST
Don't let that cloud your wide, soft eyes.
I love you and I'm faithful to my loves.
Strict ideology kills thinking—or it tries.

PEGGY
That's true—but too easy.

FAUST
Must we be believers?

PEGGY
Yes, all humans have ideology and values.
Have you read Marx, Lenin?

FAUST
Deeply long ago.

PEGGY
But didn't accept them? You somehow ran
back to this jungle law? Or didn't care.
Do you believe in purpose in life, in man?

FAUST
My darling, what can I say?
Read the deepest poets and thinkers.
Our life's a comedy or tragic play
depending on situation, vision, openness to feeling.
But "man" in abstract? That sends the senses reeling.

PEGGY
Is the universe, to you, real, material, knowable?

FAUST
What can I answer, except Yes. Yes.
My whole life's a thirst to know,
to break through illusion and routine, to press
my body to the earth, to touch, to grow.
I reject easy, glib ideals. I believe
they have no value or honest use.
They're a rusty shield to which weaklings cling
while facts and logic try to pry them loose.

PEGGY
But surely history has a promise, a goal.
We can know the past and shape the future.

FAUST
[pointing in a slow sweeping gesture to the sky]
Not yet! Look! At the limits of our minds to grasp
star clusters explode through birth and youth—
then back in blazing billion year collapse.
How strange, how dark, that final truth.

PEGGY
Each year we learn more about ourselves, about nature.

FAUST
Each scrap of knowledge is part joy, part curse.
Nothing could be better than nature—or worse.

PEGGY
That's true. But slanted toward paradox and doubt.
I heard a Party poet read something like it...
But with the dark and negative left out.

FAUST
Let each one live on his own levels.
The effort to reform people uses up our life.
Seen deeply, there are no evil forces or devils.
Fear, haste, ignorance cause all strife.

PEGGY
That sounds generous but I'm afraid
it's not useful to workers in this age.
You talk of another world, a different stage.

FAUST
You're so hopeful, so young.

PEGGY
I don't accept your friend.
He has hard eyes and a slashing tongue.

FAUST
Don't worry about it.

PEGGY
I've never known anyone as proud and cold.
And you are always together like brothers.
He seems to sway you at times—to have some hold...
and a hatred for your real nature which he smothers.
Does he care for anything but power and gold?

FAUST
Don't bother about him.

PEGGY
I always try to empathize, not judge.
But with him I can't—there's something wrong.

PEGGY (continued)

His smiles hide some secret grudge.
He thinks the rest of us don't matter or belong.
I ask myself why you travel with him,
and hope it's accidental—a passing whim.

FAUST

It takes some roughness to make a world.

PEGGY

The world his kind makes is full of death.
They're driven by a need to own and use.
He stares at each lovely thing. What will it fetch?
is his question. His life is sell, buy, win, lose.
You can see he cares for nothing living.
He tries to stand above our common life.
In his eyes the crimes are: love, softness, giving—
his presence cuts my conscience like a knife.
I'm always happy in your arms, safe...warm.
He chills me like a stabbing, winter storm.

FAUST

You care too much about everything.

PEGGY

I know it affects both you and me.
When he's around you grow confused and cool.
I have to protect myself. I even see
how to him we play the willful and the callow fool.
I won't accept his loveless life. I don't fit.
Nor do you deeply—which you won't admit—

FAUST

Sweetheart, he's not important. He can't hurt us.

PEGGY

I must leave now.

FAUST
You're always working or with your friend.
When will we have two weeks alone?
There's sun and softness now, but summer will end.

PEGGY
Carol condemns your work with City Hall.
She's suffered so from their brutality and rage.
But I trust you. When you're gone I feel the crawl
and emptiness of time. Next month when she has saved
the money for her trip—we'll have the weeks we've craved.

FAUST *[trying to give her money]*
Lend her this. Say it's money you put aside.
If she wants, she can pay it back.
Our life together will start—we'll sleep, we'll hide.
They'll be sunrises, sunsets—we won't keep track.

PEGGY
She's closer to me than a mother and more kind.
Is it safe? Can I take your word?

FAUST
Would I hurt you? I'd rather be crippled or blind.
[He presses the money on her.]

PEGGY
When I hear you, touch you, I'm so strangely stirred
I take chances. For deep reasons you're what I need.
In your presence life takes on a glow.
I listen and come to you—am I captured—or freed?
[She kisses him tentatively, tenderly. She leaves.]

SMITH *[entering]*
The young chit has gone?

FAUST
You've been poking and sniffing again?

original photo from *Soviet Film Encyclopedia*

Peggy: "I listen and come to you — am I captured or freed."

SMITH

I heard the famous professor quizzed. I hope you passed.
Perhaps you learned something—that's hard to believe.
Once more your soul was buffeted, your tongue outclassed.
From the cradle these demure ones can all deceive.
They test now for "kind hearts" and "easy ways."
Which means: can I shape and guide him all his days?

FAUST

You cold brute! Can't you ever admit
or understand motives softer than yours?
Here's a woman so generous she's unfit
for this life of grasping and greed. But she endures.
And acts against it, struggles, tries.
You use, and mock, and laugh at human cries.

SMITH

Your super lust is blowing mightily. While she blows
this mere young girl will lead you by the nose.

FAUST

You're hopeless, blind, corrupt.

SMITH

She feels that we've a quarrel—very old.
She can't abide me. I speak too hard.
She thinks evil is simple: power, gold.
I say it's at the core—all "perfection" is marred.
Health—and honesty—is seeing clear and acting bold.
So it's tomorrow that our door's unbarred?

FAUST

For me. Don't let it concern you.

SMITH

It must. I set you up. I'll see you through.

END OF SCENE 16

SCENE 17
At the Laundromat

LIZ
Have you heard about Diana?

PEGGY
Not for several weeks.

LIZ
She's making a fool of herself—
so Sybil says. Over a man.
Diana—believe that if you can.

PEGGY
How?

LIZ
How do you think?
Days off, flitting about, drink.

PEGGY
Poor Diana.

LIZ
Poor Diana, indeed. She'll get her just dessert
if that's all she thinks that life's about.
She'll have a man to play beneath her skirt
but he'll get old and bald, and bored and stout.
Then she'll wish she had her friends
who struggle together for justice and rights.
Men court you, praise you, fool you—for their own ends.
Sooner or later it ends in boring fights.
There's nothing but comradeship and work
to give your life meaning and direction.
We've no right to procrastinate or shirk.

PEGGY
Don't you have any sympathy for her?

LIZ

Sympathy! When you and I work all night
she's in bed with him or on the beach,
their hands and heads together, laughing, talking light.
The problems back here forgotten—beyond the reach
of their babble, and vivid but vulgar dreams.
Women like that you can't respect or trust.
Their work means less to them than personal schemes
for "love," or pleasure, or just simple lust.

PEGGY

They may be happy...in love.

LIZ

Does that ever last or get better?
Happy? For how long? And doing what?
She'll "help us sometimes"—when he'll let her.

PEGGY

You're too hard on her.

LIZ

That kind of love is all illusion.
I've seen too many of her "tender"type.
Their speciality is hope—then deep confusion. *[She leaves.]*

PEGGY

I could talk like that once—almost.
I wanted personal life to be a part
of work shared. I needed to help others the most
or thought I did. I'd laugh to see the start
and turnings of tangled, intense affairs.
I was "reliable," my life pleasant and steady.
Now I'm tortured by guilt, fears, cares—
I'm losing friends. I feel purposeless, petty...
Oh, but the sweetness, the deep need, the beauty.
Was I born just for sacrifice and duty?

END OF SCENE 17

SCENE 18
A People's Clinic Office

Peggy stands beneath a large photograph of Rosa Luxemburg.

PEGGY
Oh, comrade, sister,
your wide, soft eyes speak love.
And yet you were willing to give
your whole being. You put the future above
your very body. That tomorrow's children might live
you had none of your own flesh.
Could you understand a fool like me,
who was dazzled by dreams and the bright mesh
of talk that shifts and swirls like the sea.
First Carol jailed, then crippled for life
because I wasn't there, because his friend
commands the police, because in this strife
of classes you cannot love, or even bend
from rigid purpose without causing harm
to those who need you most. I failed her.
I failed them all. For the promises and charm
of one uncertain man. I let him stir
my childish imaginings and hopes.
Now I'm alone with too much guilt,
my memories tightening on my breast like ropes,
my self-respect lost—the life I had built—
all shattered—my friendships—my work.
They think I betrayed them. I don't sleep.
Behind each thought pain and darkness lurk.
I relive each wrong decision. I weep.
I have no one to talk to, no place to turn.
Each day gets lonelier and when at night
no more tears can flow my cheeks still burn.
But would I do it over? Which way is right?
I thought of you, your life, your kind eyes.
Would you have forgiven me, or stood above,
aloof, condemning, not hearing my cries?
Rosa, understand, be kind—we all need love.

END OF SCENE 18

SCENE 19
Street Near Peggy's Apartment

Night.

CRAIG *[Peggy's brother, a radical student]*
When they'd discuss systems and ideals
I'd hear them out and smile. I could wait.
One, a stoic, would say he feels
immune to chance or suffering or fate,
being part of every plant or cloud.
One wrestling wisdom from science says life
is swift but sweet and man the proud
pinnacle and purpose—that savagery and strife
just serve to sharpen the thirst, the upward thrust.
I'd stroke my beard and say, "They do some good.
But only the revolution builds human trust
and makes us care and reach out the way we should."
I'd cite my sister, her courage, her work,
her sacrifice, her gentle charm.
I'd win those arguments though some would smirk
in cynical bad grace and hope "no harm"
would come to Peggy "and her superhuman goals"
—then make bad jokes about the flesh and power.
Now perfection's pulled apart and chaos flows
like stinking floods of mud. Only fools think a flower
anything but a well-painted weed—or so it seems.
If money turned her head, then who's immune?
Ideals just mask secret, selfish schemes.
Each waits one special piper to call his tune,
then scrambles down the mountain like a rat—or child.
It hardly matters which, both are mere animals, ruthless, wild.
But what comes sneaking into view?
If he's the one I'll break his head.
He's not alone—but there are only two.
I'll strike twice and leave these vultures dead.

FAUST
[entering with Smith and looking upward]
I feel vaguely guilty and unsure.
That searchlight widens into nothing
from its blinding source. Is there a cure
for my restlessness and infinite desire
that would leave me more useful? And less a liar?

SMITH
I feel like a tough tomcat
prowling the fire escape on a summer night.
Hungry and lustful. Good. I go with that.
Each natural yearning must be right.
Each rule's a bony enemy of delight.
I feel the blood and money about to flow.
May 1st, WE'LL PURGE 'EM NIGHT, Law Day, is tomorrow.
The chance for craven legal louts to glow—
and gloat of getting rich on human sorrow.

FAUST
Once that day honored struggle, compassion, change.
Now the opposite. I find it bitter—and strange.

SMITH
Strange, hell. Each society and man grows thick,
and stiff, and stately—'til they finally die.
Go with life. Relax. The single trick
for joy is: parrot every popular lie.

FAUST
Not for me. Though I'm now less sure
of how deep our sickness is. Or its cure.

SMITH
That's halfway to wisdom. When you arrive
you'll relish my worldly work and thrive.

FAUST
For now I need your help. If she'll agree
I'll take her on some long, lazy cruise.

SMITH
It's childish of you to pay the price
for her odd guilts and inability to choose.
The night is full of stars and life.
I'll give you a tune, masculine and complete
with subtleties to snip off mushy strife
—and trick her back to worship at your feet.
[sings and plays the guitar]

LIKE ALL THE FAIR MAIDENS
WHO'VE LAID DOWN BESIDE HIM
SHE KNEW IN HER HEART THAT HE LIED.
BUT NOTHING THAT I COULD HAVE SAID
COULD HAVE SAVED HER
NO MATTER HOW HARD THAT I TRIED.
'CAUSE SHE'LL OFFER HER SOUL
TO DARKNESS AND DANGER
OF SOMETHING THAT SHE'S NEVER KNOWN.
AND OPEN HER ARMS
AT THE SMILE OF A STRANGER
WHO'LL LOVE HER AND LEAVE HER ALONE.

TOO LATE YOU'LL DISCOVER THE DEVIL
(WHO'S EVERYTHING THAT I AIN'T)
HIDING INTENTIONS OF EVIL
UNDER THE SMILE OF A SAINT.
ALL HE'S GOOD FOR IS GETTING IN TROUBLE
AND SHIFTING HIS SHARE OF THE BLAME.
AND SOME PEOPLE SWEAR HE'S MY DOUBLE.
AND SOME EVEN SAY WE'RE THE SAME.

CRAIG
[striding rapidly from the shadows to confront them]
You bastard! You come to gloat.
I'll teach you the new law.
No matter how many cops you own
we leave you in the gutter without a claw.
[He dances around Smith waiting for an opening.He then seizes the guitar from Smith and smashes it on the pavement.]

SMITH
There goes that guitar's last jangled moan.

CRAIG
Your head will make a more hollow groan.

SMITH
Faust, don't run, or turn your back!
This kid is crazy with hate and hope.
You teach him to fake and hack.
I'll teach him manners—and how not to cope.

CRAIG
[trying to attack Smith with karate but being parried]
Take that!

SMITH
Why not? Nothing to it.

CRAIG
Try this.

SMITH
Surely.

CRAIG
The son of a bitch is trained.
A master. I'm in trouble.

SMITH *[pretending to be hurt]*
Faust, help me. I showed you how.
[He and Faust strike Craig simultaneously, breaking his neck.]

CRAIG *[falling]*
Shit!

SMITH
Finally Big Mouth is quiet.
I could fix it with any cop
but papers peddling the sanctimonious tear
leak out sacred things—like names and prices—and interfere.
Now, let's get out of here!
[He and Faust leave.]

MARTHA *[at the window]*
What's going on? Stop!

PEGGY
Get a flashlight!

MARTHA
Damn teen-age brawlers.

CROWD
Somebody's been murdered.

MARTHA *[coming outside]*
Were the killers caught?

PEGGY *[following her, running]*
Who's hurt? Who's hurt?

CROWD
It's your brother.

PEGGY
My God! What horror!

CRAIG
Am I dying? So suddenly it's cold.
Don't just wring your hands and weep.
[He is trying to hold on to a wall but slowly slipping down.]
I'm freezing. Nothing's firm enough to hold.
[He is on the ground.]

CRAIG (continued)

Draw closer for some words to keep.
Sweet Peggy you're still spunky and pert.
But not as smart as I could hope.
Since you've chosen to roll about in dirt
don't stop with the first slob you rope.
Go on to others, older, even more rich
and make yourself a well-rewarded bitch.

PEGGY

My brother, my comrade, such words for me!

CRAIG

Forget the revolution and relationships. Be free.
What we did is destroyed, gone...
Now it's groping, groveling, tomorrow...tomorrow...
You started with one as quietly as the dawn.
One's only enough to earn you scorn and sorrow.
But when a dozen have used you and paid
you'll have confidence, money, no common cares.
They'll tell their cronies. Your position's made.
You can strut, and snarl, and beat down stares.
I foresee your swift and steady rise.
The weak who need you can weep or sneer.
But makeup will give you mysterious eyes
and riches buy respect—and smother fear.
You'll lead a poodle on a silver chain,
own apartments, wear severe French clothes—
have a hard mouth from ignoring pain,
but delicate perfumes to trick the nose.
You'll catch a devil—a police-protected hood.
or—if you're cagey, ambitious, cool,
a God—a Du Pont with the CIA to intrude
to murder whole countries to cement his rule.
But don't feel for others, or for me, don't brood—
it's the gutter for a sorrowing, fragile, fool.
Since you sell your body for a price
be sure to turn your soul and heart to ice.

MARTHA
You sound like a cynical, crazy man
striking blindly without cause or plan.

CRAIG
You sloppy slut! I'd strike you dead
if I weren't crippled and probably dying.
You fat bitches live for food and bed
and specialize in the lazy forms of lying.

PEGGY
[hands over her eyes, twisting and turning about in anguish]
My brother, this is agony.

CRAIG
Agony to you. Then what to me?
Spare me your quick-drying tears.
It's him you love—and his blood-stained gold.
Nothing alive is what the surface appears.
It's getting dark. It's deadly cold.
[He dies.]

END OF SCENE 19

SCENE 20

Haymarket Square

MAY 1ST. A RALLY BY LEFT GROUPS TO HONOR THE MEMORY OF THE WORKERS KILLED HERE BY THE POLICE.

Peggy is by herself, among hundreds. She feels isolated and left out. The voices we hear are probably strictly from her imagination (they are all in a woman's voice quite like hers), though it is not impossible that some of the people there are aware of her and have rejected her.

VOICES

How different she was then,
direct and certain,
part of this—
singing, feeling, loving,
working without rest,
childlike, completely at one
with life, life, all life. Her,
Peggy!
[pause]
Now poisoned thoughts,
poisoned action,
doubt.
Friends betrayed, a brother.
Isolation, doubt,
loneliness, and lies.
Selfish, sickness, sin,
soul and body torn.
Separation, guilt,
doubt, doubt, doubt.

PEGGY

I'm completely alone.
I wish I could control
my thoughts, my feelings.
Or even understand, or just accept.

CROWD *[singing with great fervor]*

SOLIDARITY, SOLIDARITY.
SOLIDARITY FOREVER.
THE UNION MAKES US STRONG.

[At this point the master of ceremonies, Studs Terkel, reads from one of Vanzetti's last letters.]

M.C.

"If it had not been for these things I might have lived out
my life talking at street corners to scorning men..."

VOICES

You'll pay now, always.
You'll reap the poison weeds
you've sown. The graves
are never silent.
You'll see their faces,
you'll hear their voices.
What you'll never have is
peace, or love.

PEGGY

I shouldn't have come here.
The words, the singing,
take my breath,
break my heart,
remind me, remind me...

M.C.

"Never in our full life could we hope to do such work
for tolerance, for justice, for man's understanding of
man as now we do by an accident..."

PEGGY

I feel light-headed.
It's all so beautiful, so large,
the sky, the people.
I'm small and hopeless.
I'm getting ill.

VOICES
She doesn't belong,
here or anywhere,
not anymore.
Never. Never.

M.C.
"Our words—our lives—our pains—nothing..."

VOICES
Real people despise her.
She works for them—
the cowards, the robbers.
Probably, probably.
She should leave.

M.C.
"The taking of our lives..."

PEGGY *[staggering—the day is very hot]*
Help me, someone.

[Several people near her come to her aid and treat her very tenderly. The music of "Solidarity Forever" plays on.]

END OF SCENE 20

SCENE 21
Long Island Mansion
(Faust Dreams of Chicago)

A large, handsome bedroom. On the walls are two richly framed oil paintings. Both of the figures in the paintings bear a striking family resemblance to Smith. One is of a gaunt, hollow-eyed, scowling general of the Mexican-American war. The other is of a fat, smiling banker of the 1920s. It is near morning. Faust and a young woman are asleep in a large bed. The blinds are open and in the distance is the faint outline of the towers of New York. As the first light reaches the bed the woman wakes, rises, and moves gracefully to the windows. She is tall, slim, beautiful. For a few moments she looks out, stretches luxuriously, and hums "East Side, West Side," to herself. She then closes the blinds and leaves the room without even looking at Faust. The stage is almost completely dark. Faust is dreaming of his recent past in Chicago.

The following four sub-scenes are alternately realistic and surreal as Faust's dream and depth of sleep change. The first and third (a street scene and helicopter above the city) are outdoors and the lighting is successively for daylight and nighttime, while the actions, gestures, clothes, etc. are completely natural. The second and fourth (City Hall, and Executive House)are indoors and nightmarish. The aldermen, for example, are distorted animals—and so are the assorted toadies, rich men, politicians at the Executive House. Their movements and gestures are wild and obscene (where called for).

SMITH
The mayor's limousine is ours if you'd like.
I'd even corral a clattering cab—
the council chamber's half an hour's hike.

FAUST
Let's walk. There are no hills and nothing's drab.
There bustling streets are full of belief
and tension, and something twisted but real
that mocks timidity, terror, grief.

FAUST (continued)
This elation and energy can heal
old jungle wounds. Even these dull years
of drugs and deadness, and dying hope
will be a wind that rips through and clears
out all flabby fraud so we can grope
for lives with less fever and tears.

SMITH
I know the opposite is completely certain.
I smell the winter waiting for these fools.
Look at them laughing, rushing. What a flimsy curtain—
that fog of "hope" that keeps them blind. These tools
of we who know, and have, and risk, and use.
This will always be my city and Daley's and Capone's.
These asses dream a bit and struggle and swiftly lose.
We toss 'em sports events, and flags, and other bones.
[He sees and greets a strutting, drunken little man.]
And here's His Honor's jackal, Jack the Lip.
Come on, my sharp-toothed slasher, give me your arm.
Point out each slippery shyster judge who'll gladly rip
all law and life to shreds for samples of my…charm.
[He makes the gesture of rubbing money in his fingers and then dropping it into a waiting palm.]

JACK MATAGAIN
[who is drunk and also bubbling with excitement at being recognized and spoken to by Smith]
Mr. Smith! 'Ish so good, sir, to see you back.
I'll show each paid-off pompous, pawn we own…
Excuse my zig-zag talk. Ish balance, I think, I lack.

SMITH
You're like the human race. It seems I've known
Dick "Hood-Robin," your boss, a million years.
His illogic, lies, grunts don't hurt my ears.

MATAGAIN
You're his grail of gold—therefore his God—I know.
So I'll guide you the little that I can.
But you have ways to wash our dirty dough.
So *you* show *me* when you spot a building or a man
you want seized or smashed. We'll strike the blow.

[They stride down North Side and North Loop streets together, almost arm in arm. Smith is in the center. The following three speeches are all in raised voices to overcome the traffic and street noises. They are all delivered in a sort of happy rush—Faust of wonder and expectation, Smith of power and worldly wisdom., Matagain of cheap booze. Matagain also flaunts his borrowed might by pushing and sneering at passers-by.]

FAUST
Look at the climbing cranes—they're new.
They brood above the buildings and seem
like toys or Martian birds that hew
and bite. Are these frantic flurries of man a dream—
or nightmare? Benefiting all, or the foxy few?

SMITH
It's part of his need for cycles and change.
He gets no tang or taste from things that last
so we help him arrange and rearrange.
He swirls about—puff, his life is past.
But we turn a profit. I call it natural, not strange.

MATAGAIN
You'd laugh or leer at what we knock down:
old stony, mossy buildings, "landmarks," giant trees...
Each new builder pays—or we cut up the clown.
How smooth it goes. We rip around and off with ease.
The fix is everywhere: commentators, colleges, cops.
We're even bringing back religion and respect:
the people in their place—worshiping painted props—
so we can specialize in—lie, bribe, collect.

CITY HALL

[They arrive at and enter City Hall. Smith is now in elevator shoes so that he is seven feet tall. As the aldermen (animals) waddle or swagger in, each bows and nods to Smith and points him out to the others.]

SMITH *[confidentially to Faust]*
This is the famous zoo that rules a city.
And here my hustlers come hopping in:
Vito Marginman: mite's brain, no trace of pity,
machine gun hidden, knuckles on floor, ugly as sin.
Pukeupski, Roman—deadly, determined, dumb.
Mr. Holeman, Mr. Clipper, Mr. Stinkbird.
Each screeches, "Hood-Robin, thanks" for every crumb.
And Crooked Tom, the cock-eyed collie of the herd.
Notice around each small, smelly head are flitting
fifty squirrel mice with steel teeth.
From these sixty fix-mad fleas go hitting
seven suckers for their dough or skin. And so we reach
a million! Thus the blood and booty all flow
up from the poor to make the city go—and glow.
Don't look so worried—it's all been blessed
by paid professors, pip-squeaks, profiteers, Rome...
These are my pimps and pawns—my perfect, antiperfect poem.

FAUST
Am I drugged, dreaming, or dead?
This is sicker than I could believe.
These dregs and dreary Dumpling Dick all fed
on human sweat and sorrow. I want to leave.
If this is your working weighty world, I'm not ready.
These bastards! Boasting, brutal—and yet so petty.

SMITH
You wanted not riches but "reality direct."
This is how man lives always, everywhere.
Hurry—our chopper—Executive House—the silly, the select.
They're cheering our scams and clapping for us there.

HELICOPTER ABOVE THE CITY

[They enter the helicopter and fly over the city.]

FAUST

Now the fog and smoke seem fragments of dawn.
They finger the crevices of concrete like light
and snake along the river. Look again it's gone—
nothing but the brutal, perfect night.
But then fog floats back again wispy, wild,
from nowhere and everywhere it glides and gilds
the rawness to beauty and the sores to mild
memories of sores. It clings, climbs, builds.
The expressways seem necklaces of light
on a sleeping breast of mud and stone.
Down there, look...one building burns marble white,
outfacing everything to set a tone
of centralness, cockiness, calm. Do I see
a rainbow spray of searing sparks?
The whole city seems alive and free
when you whirl above tenements, bright buildings, parks.

SMITH

King Mammon whom they worship spares no expense
to dazzle and divert all tourists and fools,
but keeps the slaves behind a fancy, flesh-tearing fence
of skin color, and money, and snobbery, and slick rules.

EXECUTIVE HOUSE

[The helicopter has landed. They have left it and are walking on the roof of the Executive House. Smith takes Faust to the edge of the roof.]

FAUST

The wind is like a hurricane.
My face is burning. I can hardly hear.

SMITH
Grab this gilded railing. Let me explain
these sleepless stable streets of power and fear.
[pointing to a giant publishing house across the street]
Right down...there...an idealistic, iron-faced old man
is ripping down a forest ten miles wide
with a fountain pen, by mistake to fit a plan
already obsolete. When challenged, out of pride
he'll persist and win a stalemate to mask
the folly of his flunkies. I hear the axes ring,
the great trees falling, and see the stacks
of money flowing, round the earth. The loggers sing
as they ride the great turning trunks.
And I sing too, riding the riders and that strange,
worried old man who goes home, plunks
his carcass in a soft bed and dreams of change.
But nothing can change, not folly, not fun,
not selfishness. Only a place, or face, or name.
Come into the temple—the party has begun.
Nothing is lacking—except fear and shame.
[They enter a ballroom.]

CHORUS *[greeting Smith and Faust]*
FOR HE'S A JOLLY GOOD FELLOW.
SMITH'S A JOLLY GOOD FELLOW, SURE
HE'LL GIVE US A GOLDEN CITY, PURE—
DRIVE OUT THE WORTHLESS, SNIVELING POOR.
THEN FART IN THEIR FACE SO DALEY CAN SAY,
"WUNNERFUL. NOW FOLKS, FOR SUCH BLESSINGS YOU'LL PAY."

SOLO
Here comes Smith with his speech-writing cow.
We'll get tips, truth, and a cover story now.

CHORUS
WHEN HE'S AROUND, LIFE FLOWS BY FAST
THINGS SHOOT DOWN, UP, AROUND—STONE, FLESH.
HE'S A FATHER. AND AN OLD SLY *MOTHER* TOO
WHO UNWEAVES AND WEAVES THE SACRED MESH...

VOICE
How did ya ever make it here?

[The new rich in tuxedos are drunkenly explaining their sources of wealth to each other.]

VOICE
Through Cicero.
I did time for a boss gorilla there.
Hot damn, how he could swear and glare!

VOICE
I see he made you rich.

VOICE
His gal gave me the syph.

FIRST SILVERSMITH
[These silversmiths resemble Smith in mannerism but they are much smaller, dressed in silver tights and naked from the waist up. They are lively, spontaneous, honest. The "devil" has taught man to mock—hoping to make him cynical and amoral. But the "God" in him merely uses this "devil's lesson" to mock what must be mocked, the cynical and amoral, i.e. the rich and the powerful and their flunkies.]
This is the first generation of dough:
swindlers, murderers, everything direct.
Their grandsons will be proud to show—
passed on loot, made legal, made correct.

SECOND SILVERSMITH
The women here are cold as hell,
stooped over with diamonds, furred in July.
Painted, and pampered, and hiding in shell,
outdoing their males, they rob and they lie.

THIRD SILVERSMITH
They lie like lawyers and chisel and cheat.
At poison and plotting they've never been meek.

THIRD SILVERSMITH (continued)
But they lack male madness for <u>Hell's</u> full-furious heat:
[All three silversmiths make the gesture of a mushroom cloud—twice.]
Super murderer Harry—two cities, one week.

VOICE
[to a small, prissy, stiff homosexual male who is following lovingly behind a huge, bloody-handed and bloody-shirted red-faced sheriff or warden]
Speak up for the tweeners, party-giving boy.

VOICE *[Truman Capote]*
I'm patriotic, prissy, pure, and so prim.
I'd produce a progeny as precious as I
...'cept try as I might I can't fertilize—him.

[The chaos and near orgy go on for a few minutes so that the next chorus is not too direct and simple a response to the last speech, but to the scene as a whole.]

CHORUS OF THREE SILVERSMITHS
THE WIND IS HUSHED, THE STARS ARE HIDDEN,
THE MOON OF SPRING PROMISED IS STRANGELY STARK.
THE SWIFT, SWEET RAIN LIKE LIFE FORBIDDEN
WHISPERS, WHIMPERS, THROUGH THE DARK.

[There is a storm raging outside and a pounding on the door. The mob occasionally becomes aware of the former and gradually, increasingly of the latter.]

VOICE *[from outside the door]*
Wait, help, listen.

[They are forcing the door open.]

VOICE *[from the crowd]*
Who's getting so pushy?

BLACKS
[A mixed group of blacks, of all ages and classes: wild kids, young men and women in afros, middle-aged men in business suits, old women in shawls have pushed their way in.]
Look at us. We've been sweating three hundred years
and all we have is hand-me-downs.
We hear your chants, and songs, and cheers,
and want to join such godly, happy clowns.

VOICE *[from the center of the crowd]*
If ya can't bribe and bully up like us,
don't complain. So see V.P. Spiro—bring cash
or else back down. And don't make no fuss.
[getting angry]
For the demands of the damned: the lie, then the lash.

BLACKS
[slowly retreating before the numbers and hatred of the crowd]
We worked and waited, and thought and tried.
We survived their savagery—we struggled through.
The old dream within us slowly died.
Will patience and pleading ever make things new?
[They leave.]

CHORUS
[of several of the crowd who are increasingly angry that the blacks even dared to presume and that their revels were interrupted]
Back to our boasting, and legends, and lies.
The strip-off, the rip-off, the smash in the ribs.
PISS ON THE PUBLIC, that chant never dies.
[They start to throw things at and spit at the door through which the blacks entered and left.]
Poison paint on their walls, and rats in their cribs.

FIRST SILVERSMITH *[mockingly]*
When money's the God the temple is full.
The priest is chanting, "faith, fear, follow each law."
Meaning: oblige the brute owners. For shooting such bull
we call him Cardinal or Congressman and grease his cold paw.

SMITH

[Looking for and calling out to Faust because he wants to disassociate himself from some of the excesses of the crowd, and because he fears and resents the possible influence on Faust of the silversmiths—who leave as he approaches after staring at him for a long moment—taking his measure. When Smith speaks, he is commenting on the scene around them which has grown quiet but tense.]

They push and pose, and preen and primp.
Foolish and fake they swirl about
'til slowly their silly stiffness goes limp,
and empty and exhausted they settle and pout.
Stay near me or you'll be confused:
not learning and enjoying how idiots are used.

FAUST

I'm over here.

SMITH

We were pulled apart by fools.
And this is my ballroom, my home.
[pushing through a cluster, toward Faust]
Make way, you peasants, King Roustabout needs space.
Come on, we'll leave these louts and roam
the fringes of folly for a fresh face.
This blather jars my ear too, as you might know.
But there are circles within circles here for fun.
Let's head for that antique fireplace's glow
and watch how the world's rackets are run.

FAUST

You're master of every irony, of course.
To come *here* on May Day, "Law Day," Walpurgis night—
future, present, past—reduced to naked force...
I go with you...unlearning wrong and right.

SMITH

We'll push toward the hum, and noise, and heat.
No one's alone when he schemes for stakes
of power. That's where poets and politicians meet.

FAUST
I'd rather understand the force that makes
witches and brutes of women and men.
I'd know then why the child's heart breaks,
the chance of changing my life, and how, and when.

SMITH
Study the game. Study the stakes.
Leave analysis of motives to monks.
Leave changing the world to fanatics and fools.
The clever man accepts and sings, and clunks
out praise for his sub-circle of routine and rules.
Right here are young women graceful, nearly nude,
and older ones discreet and subtly wise.
Not to pursue them marks a man a prude
cut off by fear and conscience—those tangled lies.
(Listen to that damn cello whining of bad dreams,
and the violins wringing out memory and guilt—
I hate those notes.) Right here life teems
and pleasure flows and everything we've built
is solid and safe. Just long and live to the hilt.
This is life unashamed, natural, brash.
Can you imagine it ever changing or growing quiet?
This endless world of a room is all one lovely hash
of bullying, dancing, eating, flirting—one riot
of color and corruption and caginess, and cash.

FAUST
Will you pass as old "riches" or new "dough"
as we meet the actors in your puppet show?

SMITH
Who cares? I combine both types with zest.
If I brag of "roots," or Harvard, or ancient law,
it's with the energy of parvenus at their best
and the killer instinct of hoodlums in their raw
echo and parody of kings and creating states.

SMITH (continued)
But I'm undisguised and inwardly I never lie.
You slow academic kind hearts have buried hates
that make your empire a quiet, extra deadly sty.
Let's join cold male carping, then warm female fire.
I'll give fresh Freudian comment, if you desire.
[to some old gesturing figures huddled together at the fireplace]
Gentlemen, why stand alone and bitter?
The rest are rollicking, all caught up in life.
They jump, and bark, and scatter harmless litter.
Your hands slash air like some old, bony knife.

OLD GENERAL
Don't trust nations to care or remember.
They deny you burned far-off villages for them.
Like women they love June and hate December.
All want the flower and forget the stem.

OLD STATESMAN
We were once honored and rightly so.
Now it's only we who still hold fast.
Ours was a haughty, holy age whose afterglow
still lights these fools you see careening past.

OLD BUSINESSMAN
It's true we careened ourselves a bit
and sought to knock things down and smash the old.
And with good reason. But now we're hit
with shoves and kicks from kids grown brash and bold.

OLD AUTHOR
Who reads a book now that's mystical or mature?
I was praised as, "the mid-century Poe."
Now they read subtle stuff or stark manure.
I miss the fame and honor. And the lovely dough.

SMITH
[acting very old, bent, stiff, and creaky-voiced to parody them]
Now my flask is running dry and I'm sure
the end is near for everything worthwhile.
There's nothing at all left proud and pure.
What kind of world is it that won't worship style?

HUCKSTER WITCH
Sweet masters, don't pass me by.
I'm loaded with tried tricks that every king
and crooked concocter of poisoned pie
has used for kicks and belly laughs and to wring
the final penny from the peasant sty.
Look, these charts—the magnificent stars—
chopped up and coded with Grecian names
to tell Aunt Sadie if bingo bazaars
or soapy operas have Tuesday's brightest claims.
I've "speed" and heroin for feather-headed fools,
the Cross, the Crescent, the Star for retarded slobs.
Wise men like you employ 'em as the tools
to bribe and bully muddle-headed mobs—
to cough up money, and obey your rules.

SMITH
[flipping her a corporate stock certificate folded into the shape of a many-faceted rock, for her trinkets which he jams carelessly into his pocket]
Cousin, your junk's for poorer clucks.
I sell my suckers chunks of corporate stocks
founding a flood of chatter and flow of bucks—
my rich man's religion—on greed and paper rocks.

FAUST
I'm trying hard not to be drunk.
This is fast, and flickering, and half-way fun.

SMITH
Whatever is true quickly turns to bunk.
So what good has self-denial ever done?

[A beautiful woman swirls by, dressed in gauzy white.]

FAUST
Who is that?

SMITH
That lissome, languid trick?
That's Lilith.

FAUST
Lilith?

SMITH
Some distracted spirit. The original, eternal girl.
Stay far from the orbit of her eyes.
They and her cloud of fragrant hair
entangle men 'til all ambition dies
except to hold her twisting, trembling, bare.

FAUST *[as they approach the fringes of a dance]*
Two women there, one young, one old
seem ready and eager to dance.

SMITH
With them it's right to rush in and be bold.
There's nothing useful in a furtive glance.

FAUST *[dancing with the young witch]*
A lovely sleep once fell on me
in which I dreamt an apple tree.
Swelling on that tree were two
apples too luscious to be true.

YOUNG WITCH
You've dreamt of apples, love, desire
since Eden, caves, first fitful fire.
Still in my blessed garden grow
apples to match your bright blood glow.

SMITH *[dancing with the old witch]*
A troubled sleep once fell on me
in which I dreamt a human tree.
The tree was wildly, deeply split.
But fool I was, I fancied it.

OLD WITCH
I welcome you, my worldly knight.
I love hard truth beyond delight.
Just bring your stabbing strength until
my wild deep split is calm and still.

MECHANICAL RULE LOVER
[a fat, stiff, angry man on stilts]
How come you dance and sing and live
when I have proved this age is dead?
You ought to guard your time and give
all respect and love to me instead.

YOUNG WITCH
Why does he come here?

FAUST
He's behind every lofty lie—a frozen fear.
Celebrate or argue—he'll provide
a mechanical analysis like death.
His paper preaching's just a way to hide
from shifting subtle things with life and breath.
If you march in line (even if you stumble)
he'll be decent enough and sometimes smile.
But no human, complex moves—he'll swear and grumble
of decadence and treason—in his bloated style.

MECHANICAL RULE LOVER
Are you still here pretending to live and choose?
I've classified you each a dozen times—or two.
You defy my laws to mock me or confuse
my exact science of "Man—what he must do."
I've worked so hard to rule out color and flavor.
You muddle my maps with shameless behavior.

YOUNG WITCH
Why don't you light up, loosen up, or leave?

MECHANICAL RULE LOVER
I tell you foul, foolish folks straight out:
I won't put up with noise or let you weave
me into your fine webs of feeling and doubt.
[The dance continues, ignoring him.]
I can't convince anyone at all
but I can eke out an essay and say
my true road is narrow, and those who fall
deserve to—because they went astray.

SMITH
He'll slip off his stilts and sit his ass down hard
at a desk and dictate rules to dam up life.
Anything not cold, or wooden, or steel is barred.
It's nature and flesh he hates—he loves the knife.
[to Faust]
Why did you let that lovely lady go
who smiled and sang and led the dance's flow?

FAUST
She spoke her soul and racism and sneers
like sick white mice spewed out and hid.

SMITH
So what? In a place like this with no fakery or fear,
why worry about what beauty believed or did?
Those "mice" were useful and unifying here.

FAUST
Then I saw...

SMITH
What?

FAUST
[before the same type of picture-mirror as in SCENE 6]
This painting, part photograph, part reflection:
a young woman pale, distracted, alone.
Having lost all hope, friends, direction.
With no one to help her ease the dull drone
of memory, conscience, death. Peggy? It must be.
Suddenly my casual cruelty floods back on me.

SMITH
Pay no attention. It's the trick of art
to turn you inward groping, guessing,
then outward again with a bleeding heavy heart—
half for striking blows, half for babbling and confessing.
To your real needs you grow cold. Your instinct dies.
That's the whole fable and meaning of Medusa's eyes.

FAUST
Those eyes have seen suffering too near
without anywhere to turn for relief.
That body was the center of everything dear
and intimate and soft. I fled like a thief.

SMITH
You boob. Everyman says, "It's her. It's her",
when these vague—mere vapors make his "conscience" stir.

FAUST
What agony to see that face—what joy.
Whatever calls us to love is never blind or too late.
It's other pleasures that pale and cloy.
She's all I need though I feel the weight
of the world against us, custom, fear, hate...

SMITH
A woman like her is fragmented and lost:
heart on the sleeve—house and home in a knapsack,
knowing the value of everything, never the cost.

SMITH (continued)

Her victims are piled in a mountainous stack.
Come on, New York, the clasping, coiling, center-piece is waiting:
our gold fountain where nothing is dry or cold.
There with scheming, screwing, creating,
you can't be bored—and won't grow old.

DILETTANTE HISTORIAN

[Ted White-Wash: plump, soft ,bald, fawning. He is dragging around a portrait of Richard Nixon with a white wig and the unfinished bottom section like the Gilbert Stuart portrait of Washington]

Yes, where our great country's future and behind are one.
At least I can't tell which end is which.
This sleazy crook...isn't he...Richard Washington—
(one more presidential book and I'll be rich).
It's a circus of a city where a grubby, gray guy
can dearly sell his soul if he's the itch
and end up famous—and filthy rich.

SMITH

[to Faust and audience as the lights come up]

I'm glad you know this is all a dark dream.
Such flabby fools don't fit my scheme.

[He pushes Ted White-Wash away, and sprinkles the huckster witch's trinkets on his head. White-Wash examines each one with great seriousness and reverence.]

END OF SCENE 21

SCENE 22
Long Island Mansion

Faust, who has been dreaming in the darkened room, wakes abruptly. He goes to the window and at first looks at the city in the distance around the edge of the drawn blind as he thinks or remembers the poem. Near the end he gradually opens the blind until at the end the room is flooded with the light of morning. At the end he is wide awake, active, nervous—about to leave the room and find Smith—and Peggy.

New York, on stone, on stone,
mad stalk of glass
and steel. What Dutch
Captain could guess?
Even Hamilton tough
as Romulus might pause
at what bright, foul,
elaborate silk rags
the body goes in. The core
was energy coiled like pain.

The River Drives at night—a silver ring—
the tourists sentimental, safe, pretend
there was a marriage and all the Sammy Glicks
and all the Daisy Millers lay down their heads
together on this rock pillow with no regrets.
The light will say: what of these hurt,
their haste, their blinded tears—this swarm?
The tourist is gone. The slum is stone.
In that hard face the yellow dresses of kids
squirming in the dream and blood are still
the color of baubles in the hair of immigrants
dressed up to celebrate Eden, Eden.
And the gaunt, empty, noiseless, windows of pensioners
not wanted by family, or state, or God, are hollow eyes
and what the other end of dreams involve.
This tunnel of love is blind. We count
nothing here but energy and youth.

Have we done badly or well? Only fools
would answer. I would say: Tell me what is man?
What are cities for? Work? Books? And since
you cannot really answer that question except
by the cut of your own life, by 50,000 choices
or seeming choices involving every decision, every hour
of leisure, every smile or frown, I say:
you decide. Balance the glory and the raw wound.
One word: self deceit and callousness are the price
of lies. One euphemism poisons the well.
One glib and cold assumption disqualifies the voice.
There was a politician spoke of "our African immigrants."
As if a little calculated balm would wash
the terrible holds of the slavers. As if the sharks,
the relentless sharks, leaping in their wake
would glide away. No. Not those ships and sharks,
nor the Calcutta pain, the famines,
the epidemic deaths of the surplus poor
that the 19th-century rulers never noticed.
They were real. They mattered.
Ahab knew these streets and took the sea instead.

Whisper and slow kiss, the theater, the crowds, the star-
specked pavements, the accents of all the earth,
the privacy, the fresh starts, will tempt
40,000 girls each year. They
lie down in pain, or wine, or joy—one hour,
or fifty years, or not once. Let no man judge.
Wisdom or folly are in the eye
of the actor. Who but she can count
the cuttings off? The mother dying in Philadelphia,
angry and alone. The fool husband left in Gary.
The kindness, the mistakes, the dullness
back where forever the less crowded streets
gossip and sleep with their children's quarrels
and freshness. And the small talk of married old maids.
Which of you will count for all, or one, of these
and say her wrong—or right. New York is what
the flame is, and the moth will find it—
the curl of gray smoke is dark necessity—and joy.

Fame and intelligence will draw the artist. Fitzgerald
still callow, wearing his mother's lace curtain
snobberies, will grow up here. Hart Crane
will try his frail arms to push the bridges
into sun. Wolfe will find the loneliness.
And the glitter will call him. Esther. Esther Jack.
Not ready, he will curse her. None of us are ready.
Dreiser, shambling dark oak, one hundred years
too early or too late, will edit a fashion magazine
for biddies, never forgetting Carrie, the sister of us all
or the sweet, slow summers that sing to sleep the prairie
where no distractions empty the life with fullness.

In the 1930s this town was Zion. The hunger,
the soup kitchens, the anger—the money-suckers were down.
All Jewish intelligence and tender hands said, "Forget
the past, the scramble, the madness of position and place.
There is an end to that. Now man will be a brother,
will die in Spain—wherever necessary—for man."
Now Zion is Babylon again. The calf is back
in the temple. Adjustment is his holy name. Three
dull sects compete. All offer the surface of things.
For the whites' selfishness is on us like a shroud.
"No-man's" city—and like Ulysses, blameless, all can hammer down,
rebuild for strangers, new puffing games, each generation's whims.
Your shifting, slanting colors are beyond hope
or rage, beyond condemnation, beyond praise, beyond judgement.
If readiness is everything.

City of Melville and Whitman. City
of anti-Union riots. The clumping hoofs
of Washington's gray horses mix not one
echo to this cacophony of taxis and street cries.
The parliament of man is here. And Hell
right here. Is there anything better to worship
than energy—or worse? Have you found a honey,
philosophers, like the dreams of youth?
Or an antidote to the poison of what does not work?

Rejectors, sour saying singers, haters, nostalgic
old men in rooms, if you are right, the story's over.

It did not work. It could not have worked. If discipline is needed, purpose
from above, then this
is jungle still. But if evolution holds in all things
this piling up of man's a type of song.
Even the agony was prologue. On this rock
a civilization still wanting to be loved, and therefore young,
un-self-conscious like any living thing, rushes on,
breaks its own heart. Breaks stone.
And the historians will date one of these decades:
the end of chapter one—if by luck, by work, by miracle
our courage returns—our anger.

Harlem is our crime, the scar, the muted
cornets tangible with trouble, the social workers of idiot ruled sheets, the
smiling ministers in public relations photos
to show they care. Care if twelve-year-old hustlers
take on the world. Care if old black women choke
the thoughts of Ruth while tough sons
bleed away in alcohol or hate. Care three hundred
years too late if jobless, proud fathers stare,
blinded with insight at the poisonous peeling paint, and quiet satin daughters
need heroin to change
the surreal streets to a different fantasy. This year
the owner's number one boy will lead a "trouble-maker's" march.
The owners understand. Tactics. Tactics. After
the marching the clean collars retreat. 0 orators
can anything burn pale indifference for longer
than ten summer weeks? Or match, or note,
the "grace under pressure" of these hundreds of thousands
that makes Hemingway's heroes mere raucous boys? What lever
can lift twelve generations of bone-twisting rock? Who
but fools will wait another hour? Or believe
that with each child hurt or frightened
that rusty statue should weep. The rats
are rustling in the walls like leaves.

The last chapter will always be in doubt.
A battlefield strewn with bodies and broken promises. Brave
believers in justice blooming with hope—facing
defeat, terror, indifference, hate. Malcolm,
all flaming courage and compassion falls

to assassins and rots in his grave. But,
in the capitol, the clown President
is merely nicked and rises up
to lie, rob, and ruin the republic
for eight foul years. Now,
in both cities, the plutocracy rules,
two-faced, two-partied, owning everything,
controlling, killing. And yet
can the Ellis Island millions, their
sweat, their agony, their embodied hopes—
the La Guardias, the Franklin Roosevelts
come to nothing?
We can't know.

But we can know with Whitman
that here the shaping of the Declaration's great living poem —
the new humanity will be brought alive—or lost—by us. Us
newcomers, dreamers, creators, crusaders, con men,—
forever at war. "Constricted, English, half-lettered,"
Jefferson said of Hamilton's selfish schemes
that sold us to shysters and slick bankers. He saw
the savagery and sorrow they'd spread—almost foresaw
the swift "Thickening to empire, with protest
like a bubble popping and sighing out." But
that tough-minded, trouble maker fought on. Determined,
by any means necessary,
to take the country back
from the murderous hands of greed. Knowing
the "self evident" (radical) old "truths." Certain,
as we must be,
that all the questing, dreams, bloodshed,
and blind faith, were heeding
some human urge
ancient and worldwide
for equality, full equality from birth.
Whispering to them and to us,
"It is there. It can be done.
It is necessary. Believe. Arise. Go."

SCENE 23
A New York Street

A dreary, rainy day in New York. On the street Faust sees Smith ahead, walks rapidly to overtake him, and puts his hand roughly on his shoulder to turn him around and confront him.

FAUST
Driven mad with grief and guilt! In a damn "institution!" A woman so full of life that she felt every fleck of sun—behind walls with souls worn out and hopeless. You contemptible liar, you kept it from me. Go ahead, roll your eyes with hatred, then catch yourself and mock me with that self-satisfied poise. Institutionalized! To be hurt more each day by the pain around her beyond relief—at least as long as this cold jungle brutalizes everyone it can, outside and in. You confused me with its inane distractions and hid from me all news of her despair and breakdown.

SMITH
She's not the first.

FAUST
You lying dog! You and your cur are close relatives. He likes to roll around at the feet of the strong, then jump up and terrorize the weak. Yelping and circling. Turning any poor clod he can smell fear on into a trembling, begging, caricature—you too. Not the first! The thought of even one human living in that frigid, chaotic hell hurts me in my bones and makes me shake with rage. But at the agony of thousands you just shrug.

SMITH
You thought you were ready for the real world. Eager to know and understand all life and death. *One* single human sorrow unnerves you—the first thing that goes wrong. Where's the cocky Dr. Faust who insisted the universe itself and all humanities past and future were hardly enough for his great appetite?

FAUST
Don't try your shrewd subject changes on me. I never meant not to care. To become a monster like you, all cold observation and mockery—actually enjoying each example of folly and ruin.

SMITH
Are you finished?

FAUST
Help me help her or I'll break with you once and for all.

SMITH
I can't undo what's done. Who picked her out and insisted on, "her, that one, only her." Was it you or me?

[Faust looks around wildly, and moves his hands as if he wants to strike blows.]

Oh, are you looking for a lead pipe or baseball bat? It's lucky you're such an amateur at force. Otherwise you lofty, liberal loose thinkers would have killed everyone else by now—for puncturing your illusions, "talking back," telling the simple, earthy truth.

FAUST
Take me to her. I must get her out.

SMITH
Think of the risk. Her brother's friends are irrational men, capable of wild acts—rages and terror. If they knew of you, or could find you, you'd be the perfect "symbolic" victim. The late Dr. Gordon Faust, an example to all bourgeois corrupters who dare touch a revolutionary.

FAUST
You, with all your power, who supposedly can get away with anything, suddenly preaching caution! I'll take the risk.

SMITH
Fine. I can reach the authorities, of course, any authorities. Within limits we can break the rules. You can talk to her and sign her out—unless she's raving. I'll have whatever transportation amuses you ready. Then take her wherever you want. That I can do.

FAUST
Then let's go. Right now.

END OF SCENE 23

SCENE 24
A Mental Institution. The Waiting Room.

Winter. Smith and Faust in dark, expensive suits, in the huge waiting room of a bustling institution. There are: wildly flashing computer readouts; garbled, weird messages over the public address system; banks of dozen of video monitors of every room and corridor; hysterical relatives; rushing clerks; teasing, giddy nurses; pompous, stupid doctors, etc.

FAUST
What are they up to? Why does it take hours
just to see her?

SMITH
I don't know what they're doing or brewing.

FAUST
Gushing about nothing, rushing about, wheezing, teasing...

SMITH
It is an institution, a madhouse, of course.

FAUST
If only things could be redefined, and the right ones confined.

SMITH
Always you're eager, bull-headed, and unkind.

END OF SCENE 24

SCENE 25
A Mental Institution. Peggy's Room.

Late afternoon. Faust in a huge, deserted corridor outside Peggy's room. He has a key to it.

FAUST
Now, a fear I haven't felt for years—
madness from empathy with the misery of man.
She's here because that demon always rears
up and kills the sensitive if it can.
Now seeing her, I hesitate.
Can I bear her agony? To feel her tears?
Promises and love are a crippling weight.

PEGGY
[Singing, she has not heard Faust opening the door to her room, which is darkened in spite of the time of day.]
MY SISTER, THE WHORE,
HAS LEAD ME TO DEATH.
HER HUSBAND, THE MAYOR,
HE STOLE ALL MY BREATH.
MY BROTHERS HAVE SCATTERED
MY BONES ON THE SEA.
THE FUTURE THAT MATTERED
HAS ENDED FOR ME.
FORGET, FORGET, FLY AWAY FREE.

FAUST
She doesn't dream I hear her desperate singing.
Or of the companionship, the hope I'm bringing.

PEGGY
[to Faust ,whom she does not recognize in the darkness]
Nurse, why do you wake me so early?
I must rest and dream of my life.
The days are bright and long and surly

PEGGY (continued)
with selfishness, sharpness, strife.
In a new world would careless killers be hung?
I used to be so young, so young...
Now I'm tired, and old, and without hope.
And pretty they used to say. He thought so.
He'd insist, "Now deep happiness is within our scope."
His sudden leaving was the final blow.
[She turns away from him. He puts his hands gently on her shoulders and slowly shakes her.]
Nurse, don't shake me like a child.
What have I ever done to you?
The facts of my life are bloody and wild.
Let me rest here and pretend wishes come true.

FAUST *[to himself]*
Can I live with this grief, this reality?

PEGGY
I'm completely at your mercy.
In nursing that baby I did well.
I watched it and loved it all night long.
Separation from those you love is the final hell.
They say, "Don't trust her. She never did belong."
I won't ever be happy again.
Their talking strange half-truths against me...I think.
I don't know how I lost control or when.
Why should they mock—and push me toward the brink?

FAUST *[falling at her feet]*
Here's the man who loves you.
And wants you back and happy.

PEGGY
[flings herself down beside him, but looks away from him]
Let's hope the doctors can help.
I don't want to go mad.
I mustn't hear voices.

PEGGY (continued)
Daydreams are childish, or wistful, or sad,
but they preserve life, and sanity, and choices.
But I'm lost if I think I really hear him.
Without reason life's too wretched, too grim.

FAUST *[loudly]*
Peggy! Peggy!

PEGGY *[listening attentively]*
That's my sweetheart's voice!
[She is turning her head slowly toward him.]
Where is he? Show me! Show me!
Now I feel safe and free!
With his arms around me I can rest
and believe in the earth and joy again.
He called "Peggy, Peggy," his voice chased
off all guilty memories and pain.
To hear him is heaven. To hold him is too much.
On my dying day I'll know his voice and touch.

FAUST
It is I.

PEGGY
Say it just once again. You mustn't lie.
[throwing her arms around him]
It's you! It's you! Now my agony is ended!
I don't fear the future or the past.
You came for me. This day is splendid,
and sun struck, and moving too fast.
I'm confused with hope. I see the beach
where we first met and walked,
and that garden. It seemed out of reach—
that afternoon—how we chattered, and teased, and talked.

FAUST *[rising]*
Come, dear, we must leave.

PEGGY *[caressing him]*
Wait! I just want to be with you.

FAUST
We must leave.
If we wait around too long
everything will be complicated and wrong.

PEGGY
What, you've forgotten how to kiss?
My darling, gone these few weeks, this little hour
and you can't kiss as deeply as you did?
Where's the eagerness and power
that woke me, warmed me, found me if I hid
in coyness or sleep. Now I feel a fear
though we hold each other and call each other dear.
Kiss me.
Or I'll kiss you. *[She kisses him.]*
Your lips are cold
and quiet.
O God! I don't know.
Where did the tenderness go?
What has happened to me? *[She turns away from him.]*

FAUST
Come on, darling. Once we're out of here
my love will make you happy and free.
No more loneliness, guilt, fear...

PEGGY
Is it you? Is it really you?

FAUST
It is. You must come.

PEGGY
You're taking me from this place?
Do you know what a monster you're setting free?
The suffering I've caused and have to face?
The crimes and callousness that spread out from me?

FAUST
Please, darling, it's getting late.

PEGGY
I betrayed my best friend.
I led my brother into death.
We're both involved in that, I know.
You too. Is it you? It takes away my breath
to see you. Give me your hand. Don't ever go.
Your hand, my darling, is wet.
[His hand is wet from her tears.]
Wipe it off. Is it blood? Time heals things?
They say we easily forget.
Who knows what loving and sleeping brings?
Don't be angry or hasty anymore.
Your world is crowded with hatred and horror.

FAUST
Oh, let the past be past.
Wounds heal. Pain doesn't last.

PEGGY
Not for you. You go on.
But evil weighs too heavily on me.
My brother, Carol, friends, purpose, all gone.
What future can I expect to see?
When I die we'll all be together.
Until then it's loneliness, separation, grief...
He's rotting away—this wet winter weather
makes meetings and partings so weirdly brief.
New life is fragile but full of hope.
Remember that baby sleeping at my breast?

PEGGY (continued)

You brought the world in all its swirl and scope.
Loving you was my wildest hour—and my best?
But it's poisoned. It's ending. Or it should.
Now I'd have to force myself on you.
I feel you draw back—that's the clue.
Yet you're here trying to be kind and good.

FAUST

If you care about us, then come with me.

PEGGY

Out to your greed-mad world?

FAUST

To freedom. With me.

PEGGY

If that means agony,
living out your days surrounded by the dead,
I can do it here. All the woe
and withering's within me. All my blood is bled.
You're leaving here? Gordon, how I wish I could go.

FAUST

You can. There's nothing to stop us.

PEGGY

I can't leave. I have no hope.
For me, memory is a coiling, scraping, rope.
It's hell either working for them or starving.
It's deeper hell to feel guilt.
Despair is watching your love wilt.
My heart's the feast. Time does the carving.

FAUST

I'll be with you. I'll help.

PEGGY
Go backwards,
undo the killing.
I see him
as a child,
always innocent,
dreaming, wild.
He wants to live
for hope, for worth,
on this green earth.
We'd have to give
him back his body and breath.
He's crying out against death.

FAUST
If only you could understand, accept reality and pain.
We could be happy and free.

PEGGY
If only we had everything over again.
I hear Carol talking lovingly to me.
My fingers are freezing, my mouth is dry.
I hear Carol lovingly talking to me.
She always had patience. Always knew the "why."
Now she's crippled, more quiet, more cold...
It was for us she went away.
So we could love both night and day.
[She looks out the window.]
God, those icy fields were once all green and gold!

FAUST *[bluffing]*
Since you won't come, I'll call them to help me.
Anything to allow you to someday see...

PEGGY
Never! Don't do anything by brute power.
I won't be used again. Not ever again!
The wind takes the pleasure. I eat the pain.

FAUST
Dear, it's getting so late.

PEGGY
Night is coming. Yes, a bitter night.
It should have been ours just for love.
But this world's not human yet, or right
for anything but smash, and strike, and shove.
Are your friends expecting you?
Mine have sworn off me.
We'll meet again some day. Old things will seem new
like dreams. Dreams—every feeling somehow free?
Now we're both barred off from life.
I hear its jungle sounds, too sharp, too loud.
You feel almost nothing—too safe, so proud.
That's in the bed between us, and that bloody knife.
Always I'll stay here, "fragmented," and lost.
They enjoy "taking care of me," talking
bright cold nonsense about "adjustment" and "the cost
of not accepting" what I hear crippling, killing, stalking.

FAUST
Oh, why was I born?

SMITH *[entering the still darkened room]*
We'll have to leave without her.
She's beyond the reach of help or reason.
We've journeys and appointments we can't defer.
For weakness there's never a good place or season.

PEGGY *[recoiling from Smith]*
What's that monster doing here?
Hasn't he done enough to us yet?
He's the cold, dry hell I must forget.
He's crazy. The only thing he loves is fear.

FAUST *[halfway between her and Smith]*
You'll be all right, dear. You'll be well.

PEGGY
Me? Tomorrow can judge me—the unborn.

SMITH
Come on, or I'll leave you with her.

PEGGY
I belong in the world of dreams.
That's all I have or ever had.
I can't live. I hear too many screams.
Gordon, that world's so savage and so sad.

SMITH
She will always be insane.

YOUNG PSYCHOLOGIST
[quietly, but firmly to Faust]
When the world is well she will be.

SMITH
Come on, let's go.
[Faust goes with him. They close the door.]

PEGGY
[from within, as they disappear down the corridor]
Gordon! Gordon!

AFTERWORD—AS THE AUDIENCE LEAVES THE THEATRE

You got to cross that lonesome valley.
You got to cross it by yourself.
There ain't no one can cross it for you.
You got to cross it by yourself.

Human life is swift and strange.
Human purpose lies broken, still.
Can all the desert and the darkness
ever break one stubborn will?

Some say Faust was a good man.
Some say Faust was cruel.
I say Faust was a natural man,
a genius and a fool.

You got to cross that lonesome valley.
You got to cross it by yourself.
There ain't no one can cross it for you.
You go to cross it by yourself.

Human life is short and secret.
Cut and smashed each human goal.
Can all the hatred of endless winter
completely kill a restless soul?

Some say Faust was an animal.
Some say, "always too clean."
I say Faust is your brother—
the good, the evil half seen.

You got to cross (etc.)

FOR THE ACTOR WHO PLAYS PEGGY

It all turns on you, my dear.
Smith has the hard wisdom and the verve.
Evolution chiseled him lean, quick, clear
about real motives and daily fraud. The nerve
he scratches Nietzsche and Freud scratch too. The fire
he singes with sings in our animal blood.
Great Faust has wild poetry and deep desire.
Trapped, like all of us, between sky and mud,
he's both saint and fool—crazy for change.
Your small gestures decide it. Are you selfless, wise—
tomorrow's sweet child with love and revolution's range?
Or is that subtler selfishness in your bright eyes?
Each night it's up for grab. There is no answer yet.
Only in your heart does good or evil win the bet.

FOR THE ACTOR WHO PLAYS SMITH

Go get 'em, man! I'm with you.
You're the "baddest nigger" of them all.
"The Id is forever young," there's your clue.
Nothing can touch you or end your wild ball.
You're all energy, a blazing, unbroken kid.
Yet older than God, tougher surely, wiser perhaps.
Your shit detector works through marble, helps us rid
the world (I mean ourselves) of the ego's traps
so subtle, so insidious they finally kill
not just the body, but the heart, the living will.

FOR THE ACTOR WHO PLAYS FAUST

Poor bastard: no humor, little softness, much pride.
You think the world balances on your shoulders, Hell
yaps at your naked feet. Always you've fled, failed, lied...
Always you're up at dawn, working, believing. At night you tell
yourself, "I won't go on. I'll cop out, I won't care."
You go on. You care about everything—even animals and trees.
And her, the hope, the future. Until his brutal stare
destroys your lies, evaporates your wonder, twists you to your knees.
Still to her perfect gentleness—you reach out. Then jump
to his hissing tongue and the promises of adventure, greed...
You're a man who won't grow up. Or give up. You won't lump
any qualities together without argument. You think. You need
everything...nothing. You're a difficult man, a poet, a fool.
Not my brother, but me (and you)—kind, strange, cruel.

FOR PEGGY, FOR ALL WOMEN, FOR ALL REVOLUTIONARIES

Promises, promises, promises. You live on hope.
Like a hummingbird's your beauty awes and makes
it possible we'll see, care... Otherwise we grope
blind and compulsive in selfish routine. The heart breaks
to see you alone, in despair, by dreams betrayed.
But still believing in that over-turning to come.
Man will master the beast. The agony will fade.
Even personal love will be in time—for some.
But only because you knew the devil smiles and sings.
You knew how to work, and fight, and when to flee.
You knew all subtle, soft, and secret things.
And taught them subtly, softly, secretly to fools like me.

On Goethe

JOHANN WOLFGANG VON GOETHE perhaps comes as close as any man to deserving the title of universal genius. Poet, dramatist, critic, scientist, administrator and novelist, he was born at Frankfurt-am-Main in 1749, the son of well-to-do parents with intellectual interests; and he studied at the University of Leipzig and Strassbourg, where he wrote a play which initiated the important *Sturm und Drang* movement. During the next five years he practiced law in Frankfurt and wrote *The Sorrows of Young Werther*, a remarkable novel autobiographical of one side of Goethe's nature. In 1775 he went to visit the court of the young Duke of Weimar, and, except for an extended journey to Italy a decade later, stayed there the rest of his life, filling at one time or another all the major posts of the Weimar government. Here a close friendship with Schiller developed, and here he conducted important scientific experiments and published a steady stream of books of the highest order and in many different forms. He became the director of the Weimar Theatre in 1791 and made it the most famous in Europe. His life held a number of ardent loves, which he celebrated in lyrics that are compared to Shakespeare's, and in 1806 he married Christine Vulpius whom he had loved for many years.

He could not help spreading outward and upward from the mystery surrounding him, for it was the mystery of nature. He was aware of it in everything, and he felt it in himself, his friends and in the women he loved. He tried to penetrate into it by every road he could find, through poetry and by studying geology, physiology, physiognomy, the life of planets, the practical life of man and societies.

— Edwin Muir